South Africanish

Irish

Thaiish

Indianish

Italianish

Mozambiqueish

Chineseish

Mexicanish

Greekish

Americanish

Contents

ACKNOWLEDGEMENTS

Firstly a big thank you and virtual hug to my family, especially to my fabulous parents, Monica and Norman. Everyone who meets them instantly falls in love with their genuineness, generosity of spirit and humble dignity. Thank you for being so supportive and helping me make the vision I had for this book a reality. My two older brothers, Tremaine and André, I've always looked up to you as my big brothers, so I hope you are proud of this book and your recipes in it. To my two gorgeous sisters-in-law, especially Le-Ann, who is like a real sister to me. Thank you for all your support and encouragement. It's lovely to know you are thinking of me. And to my nephew Kyle and the golden girl nieces-Francesca, Hannah and Arabella-I hope I am the Cool Aunt. But besides teaching you the things that your parents won't, I hope you can learn something from the things I've done right and the mistakes that I've made as I carve my path through life.

This book began with a month of intense 5am start photo-shoots in Cape Town in order to capture the 140 images in the book.

I am so happy with the way the photographs have worked out, and I owe the quality and artistry of the images to my South African creative team. Sean Calitz, my very talented food photographer with a heart of gold, who is just a fabulous person to be around. Lisa Clarke, my gorgeous food stylist, who should be in front of the camera, not just the beautiful food she styles. And Sara Lohmaier and Josh Ness, who worked so hard to source the best ingredients and do the hard graft. It was an absolute pleasure to work with you and I was really sad to leave.

And my Dublin team, the heart of which are my designers Richard Walshe and Alan Wall from Workhouse. Thank you for smoothing over all the bumps and giving me exactly what I want in design. Well done for finding the humour in my scissors and Pritt Stick design moments! Every girl needs a good photographer to make her feel and look good, and Harry Weir is that guy. Always professional and good humoured, thank you for getting me through a Baltic photo-shoot on a wintery Irish beach. A massive thank you to my buffer and agent, Sinead Ryan, who keeps me sane and makes me laugh when I'm stressed. And most importantly, thank you for looking out for me and having my best interests at heart.

And a big thank you to the most patient and meticulous typesetter and designer, Andrea Willmore, who has had the massive task of putting together this book.

And of course a big thank you to my sponsors, without whom this book wouldn't be possible. Vincent Dolan from Total Produce, who has kindly agreed to sponsor a second book in the Ish Factor Series. Aoife Dromey and Calor Gas, who are launching an exciting Mini BBQ, the best of luck with that venture. And Adrian McLaughlin from The Gibson Hotel, who has been so generous in laying on a fabulous book launch for me and working together to create a contemporary BBQ menu for The Gibson.

And thank you to you, the reader, for picking up this book and supporting a self-published authors' dream. I hope this cookbook becomes well-thumbed and used, covered in BBQ sauce, wine stains and all the hallmarks of having a good time. From my family to yours, I hope this book gives you many years of pleasure and is the beginning of new BBQ traditions.

ix

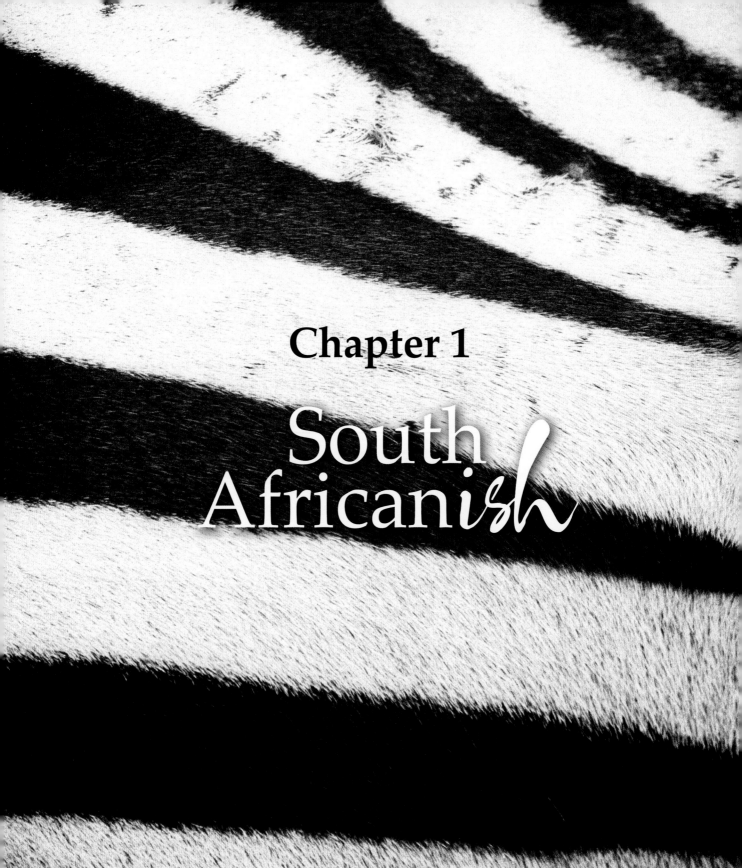

Chapter 1

South African*ish*

Boerewors Kofta and Cherry Tomato Chutney

Ingredients:

- 1kg lamb mince
- 1 onion, grated
- 1 tbsp white wine vinegar
- 2 tsp ground coriander
- 1 tsp ground allspice
- 1 tsp salt
- 1/2 tsp ground cloves
- 1/2 tsp white pepper
- 1/4 tsp ground nutmeg
- 12 rosemary branches or metal or bamboo skewers
- crusty bread rolls, to serve

Chutney:
- 2kg cherry tomatoes, halved
- 500g onion, diced
- 250ml caster sugar (use your measuring jug to measure by volume)
- 250ml white wine vinegar
- 2 tsp curry powder
- 2 tsp salt

Serves 8

Method:

1. To make the chutney, place the tomatoes and diced onion in a heavy-based pot and simmer for 20 minutes, until softened.
2. Add the sugar, vinegar, curry powder and salt. Slowly bring to the boil, stirring to dissolve the sugar. Lower the heat and simmer until the chutney has reduced and is thick and syrupy. Stir constantly! Depending on how soft the fruit is, this may take up to 1 1/2 hours. Allow to cool slightly.
3. Mix the lamb mince, onion, vinegar and spices together. Mould onto the rosemary branches or skewers in sausage shapes. Cook on a medium-hot BBQ for 3 minutes per side (about 12–15 minutes in total).
4. Serve with crusty bread rolls and plenty of cherry tomato chutney.

Coriander is a spice that permeates South African cooking, from our traditional boerewors sausage through to our cured meat speciality, biltong. The seeds have quite a different flavour from the fresh leaves. To get the most flavour, dry fry the whole seeds until you can smell them, then grind them down with a mortar and pestle or in a spice grinder.

Sticky Chicken Thighs with Prickly Pear Salad

Ingredients:

- 6 chicken thighs, either boneless or on the bone
- sunflower oil
- salt and freshly ground black pepper

Basting sauce:
- 1/2 onion, cut into chunks
- 75ml sunflower oil
- 75ml apple cider vinegar
- 2 tbsp dark brown sugar
- 2 tbsp apricot jam
- 2 tbsp Worcestershire sauce
- 2 tbsp soy sauce
- 1 tsp English mustard powder
- 1 tsp paprika
- salt and freshly ground black pepper

Prickly pear salad:
- 3 stalks of celery, sliced
- 2 prickly pears, peeled and sliced (use 200g strawberries if you can't get prickly pears)
- 2 kiwi fruit, peeled and sliced
- 100g red seedless grapes
- 50g salted cashew nuts

Salad dressing:
- 1 mango, peeled and chopped
- zest and juice of 1 lime
- 50ml (1/4 cup) rice wine vinegar
- 1 tsp sugar
- 1 tsp salt
- 1 tsp Dijon mustard
- 125ml (1/2 cup) grapeseed oil

Method:

1. Soak 12 bamboo skewers in cold water for 1 hour.
2. Mix all the baste ingredients together.
3. Lightly oil the chicken with sunflower oil and season well with salt and pepper. Using 2 bamboo skewers per thigh, skewer the chicken pieces in a cross shape.
4. Grill on a hot BBQ on all sides until well sealed and crispy. Baste liberally.
5. Move the chicken to a medium-hot part of the BBQ and continue to grill for 20–25 minutes for boneless thighs or 30–35 minutes for thighs on the bone, until cooked through. Check the thickest part of the thighs for any pink.
6. To make the dressing, blitz the mango, lime zest and juice, vinegar, sugar, salt and mustard in a blender. Gradually pour in the oil until it emulsifies.
7. Gently toss all the salad ingredients together. Divide the salad and chicken between 6 plates. Drizzle the dressing over and serve.

Serves 6

Worcestershire sauce is a world famous British condiment first produced commercially in 1837. The original recipe, or a version of it, hails from India. The recipe is a closely guarded secret, but we know includes a range of spices like cloves and mace, astringents such as tamarind, anchovies and vinegar. A few drops of this spicy, sweet, tangy, savoury sauce will add oomp to marinades, gravies, sauces, egg dishes, lacklustre veggies-just about anything.

Curried Lamb and Apricot Skewers

Ingredients:

- 500g leg of lamb, diced into bite-sized pieces (not too small)
- 200g dried apricots
- salt and freshly ground black pepper
- micro leaves or fresh coriander, to garnish

Marinade and basting sauce:
- 5 lime leaves, bruised
- 2 cloves of garlic, crushed
- 2 cloves
- 1 cinnamon stick
- 1 thumb-sized piece of fresh ginger, peeled and grated
- 1/2 onion, left whole
- 125ml apple cider vinegar
- 75ml port
- 2 tbsp apricot jam, melted
- 2 tbsp sunflower oil
- 1 tbsp dark brown sugar
- 1 tbsp medium curry powder
- 1 tsp ground coriander
- 1 tsp turmeric
- 1/2 tsp allspice

Serves 8

Method:

1. Mix all the marinade ingredients together in a large plastic or glass bowl. Reserve 4 tablespoons for basting.
2. Add the cubes of meat to the bowl and mix well. Cover and marinate in the fridge overnight.
3. The next day, soak 8 bamboo skewers in cold water for 1 hour. Cover the apricots with boiling water and soak for 30 minutes, then drain.
4. Skewer the meat and dried apricots onto the bamboo skewers. Season very well with salt and pepper.
5. Grill on a hot BBQ for 3 minutes a side, then baste well with the reserved marinade. Cook for 15–20 minutes – don't overcook the meat, as it's better when it's slightly pink. Part the meat on the skewer to see how pink it is.
6. Serve garnished with micro leaves or fresh coriander.

Allspice, often confused with mixed spice, is a secret weapon Pantry Pal. A pinch of this spice will transform meatballs, burgers, stews and BBQ sauces. It has an interesting savoury, aromatic flavour that gives food an extra dimension without being distinguishable in the overall flavour. Dried spices keep well for 6 months if well sealed, then they start losing their pungency.

Tremaine's West Coast Crayfish with Curried Citrus Butter

Ingredients:

- 4 crayfish or lobster
- 4 lemons, cut into wedges

Salad:
- 10 radishes, sliced
- 3 spring onions, chopped
- 2 heads of baby Cos lettuce, leaves separated and washed
- 2 avocadoes, sliced
- 1 papaya, sliced
- 2 tbsp chopped fresh coriander or micro salad leaves, to garnish

Salad dressing:
- 50ml (1/4 cup) extra virgin olive oil
- 50ml (1/4 cup) sunflower oil
- 2 tbsp dry white wine
- 2 tbsp lemon juice
- 1 tsp lemon zest
- 1 tsp Dijon mustard
- 1/2 tsp caster sugar
- salt and freshly ground black pepper

Curried citrus butter:
- 2 tsp curry powder
- 1 tsp English mustard powder
- juice of 1/2 lemon
- 225g butter, softened
- 2 cloves of garlic, crushed
- coarse sea salt and freshly ground black pepper

Serves 4 as a side dish

Method:

1. To make the butter, dissolve the curry powder and mustard powder in the lemon juice. Add the spice mixture to the softened butter along with the crushed garlic and a good pinch of salt and pepper. Scoop the butter onto a sheet of parchment paper. Shape into a log and wrap up in the paper like a Christmas cracker, tying the ends with string. Place in the fridge or even the freezer to slice off discs whenever needed.
2. Toss all the salad ingredients together except the coriander or micro salad.
3. Put all the salad dressing ingredients in a jam jar with a lid and give it a good shake. Dress the salad just before serving.
4. To cook the crayfish, place each crayfish on a board, belly down, tail outstretched. Rest a large, very sharp knife, down the length of the back from the small horn between the eyes. Press down or hit the knife with a mallet to split the shell neatly, then cut through the tail. Scrape out and discard the entrails. Rinse the crayfish and pat them dry.
5. Season the crayfish with salt and pepper and brush with some melted curried citrus butter. Place the crayfish flesh side down on a medium-hot grill just long enough to lightly brown the meat. Lightly oil the lemon wedges and grill until they're just charred.
6. Turn the fish, baste liberally with melted curried citrus butter and cook for a further 15–20 minutes, until the flesh is opaque and pulls away easily from the shell.
7. Serve the crayfish with curried citrus butter, charred lemon wedges and dressed salad garnished with coriander or micro salad leaves.

English mustard powder is a seasoning and cooking condiment made from ground mustard seeds, turmeric and flour. It has a strong, sharp taste that is pungent rather than hot. You can also buy it ready prepared as a paste in a jar. I use English mustard to flavour salad dressings, marinades, basting sauces and any time a little oomph is required. It's a multipurpose Pantry Pal.

Roosterkoek (Griddle Bread) with Avocado, Blue Cheese and Biltong

Ingredients:

- 1 litre plain cream flour (use your measuring jug to measure by volume)
- 20g dried yeast
- 1 tsp sugar
- 1 tsp salt
- 225ml warm water
- 2 tbsp sunflower oil

Toppings:
- 3 avocados, mashed with the juice of 1/2 lemon and seasoned with salt and pepper
- 150g blue cheese, crumbled
- 150g sliced beef biltong, Parma ham or crispy bacon
- 1/2 pomegranate, seeds only
- 4 spring onions, finely sliced
- 2 tbsp micro coriander leaves or shoots

Serves 6

Method:

1. Sift the flour, yeast, sugar and salt into a large mixing bowl. Make a well in the centre and pour in the warm water and the oil.
2. Mix the dough with your hands. Once it forms a ball, turn it out onto a lightly floured surface and knead until it's smooth and elastic.
3. Lightly oil a large bowl and place the dough in it. Cover lightly with oiled cling film and leave it to prove in a warm place until it doubles in size.
4. Knock back the dough by turning it out onto a lightly floured surface and kneading for a few minutes.
5. Divide the dough into small balls and flatten them with your hands. Place them directly onto a medium-hot grill or use a wire-hinged sandwich BBQ rack.
6. Toast well on one side, then turn them over. The bread is cooked when it sounds hollow when you tap it.
7. The traditional way to serve roosterkoek is with plenty of butter and homemade preserves. For this savoury version, top with the mashed avocado, crumbled blue cheese, biltong and pomegranate seeds. Garnish with spring onions and coriander.

Biltong is a traditionally spiced and cured meat from South Africa. It can be made from beef or venison, like springbuck or kudu. Top-quality cuts of meat are cured, spiced and dried. Biltong is sold as whole fillets or thinly sliced. Deliciously salty and spicy, biltong makes a great savoury snack and is a good source of lean protein.

BBQ Butternut Squash with Spicy Chickpea and Feta Filling

Ingredients:

- 2 butternut squash
- olive oil
- salt and freshly ground black pepper
- 125ml (1/2 cup) quinoa (use your measuring jug to measure by volume)
- 250ml (1 cup) chicken stock
- 100g chorizo, sliced
- 5 peppadews, chopped
- 1 x 400g tin of chickpeas, drained and rinsed
- 225g baby spinach leaves
- juice of 1/2 lemon
- 100g feta cheese

Serves 4

Method:

1. Halve the butternut squash lengthways and scoop out the seeds with a soup spoon. Drizzle over some olive oil and season well with salt and pepper. Wrap each butternut squash half in foil and cook in the coals of the BBQ or on a medium-hot grill for 45 minutes, until tender. Check by prodding with a dinner knife.
2. Put the quinoa and stock in a pot. Bring to the boil, then reduce to a simmer for 15 minutes, until all the liquid is absorbed.
3. Fry the chorizo in a large pan until it's crispy. Add the peppadews, chickpeas and spinach and heat through. Fluff up the quinoa with a fork and add it to the pan. Season to taste with the lemon juice and lots of black pepper.
4. Peel back the foil from the butternut squash. Spoon in the filling and sprinkle with feta cheese.
5. Serve the butternut squash wrapped in the foil to keep it warm.

Peppadews are a type of sweet, piquant pepper native to the Limpopo region of South Africa. They were first discovered in 1993 and are now readily available in jars in a sweet pickling liquid. Peppadews come in mild and hot varieties and are ideal added to a dish for a little heat without the need to use fresh chillies. A handy Pantry Pal to dolly up salads, chorizo bean stews, quesadillas or huevos rancheros or to serve with prawns or as a canapé.

Pumpkin Polenta Pap with Bacon, Leeks and Cheese

Ingredients:

- 350g pumpkin or butternut squash, peeled and diced
- 400ml chicken stock
- 1 tsp salt
- 250ml (1 cup) polenta or maize meal (use your measuring jug to measure by volume)
- freshly ground black pepper

Topping:
- olive oil
- 12 baby leeks or spring onions (ideally leeks)
- 12 pumpkin or butternut wedges or pieces
- 8 streaky rashers
- 100g grated white mature Cheddar cheese
- 100g feta cheese, crumbled
- 50g grated Parmesan cheese

Serves 4 as a side dish

Method:

1. To make the pumpkin pap, put the pumpkin or butternut, stock and salt in a large pot. Cover and simmer for 20 minutes, until the pumpkin is soft. Gradually add the polenta and stir with a wooden spoon. The mixture should be firm but not too dry. Add more stock or boiling water if it's too dry. Simmer gently while stirring until it's smooth and firm. Season with salt and pepper.
2. To make the topping, lightly oil the baby leeks and grill on a medium-hot BBQ until they're charred. Do the same with the pumpkin or butternut wedges. Grill the rashers on the BBQ until they're very crispy and golden.
3. Serve a dollop of pumpkin pap with chargrilled leeks, roasted pumpkin or butternut, crispy bacon and the cheeses. Thank me later.

Polenta is a type of finely milled maize meal that can be used in baking bread and cakes. You can also make it into a smooth paste that can be served with milk and sugar as a porridge or as a savoury side dish with herbs and grated Parmesan cheese. In South Africa, we use a coarser maize meal to make pap, a version of porridge that can be served as a breakfast porridge or as a savoury dish, often with cooked tomatoes and onion.

Monica's Hot Potato Salad with Bacon and Mustard Dressing

Ingredients:

- 1kg baby potatoes, halved
- 250g streaky rashers or bacon lardons
- 4 eggs
- 6 large dill pickles or gherkins, sliced, or baby gherkins
- 6 spring onions, sliced
- 2 tbsp finely chopped fresh flat-leaf parsley
- crème fraîche, to serve (optional)

Dressing:
- 1 clove of garlic, peeled and left whole
- 4 tbsp olive oil
- 2 tbsp apple cider or white wine vinegar
- 1 tbsp wholegrain mustard
- salt and freshly ground black pepper

Serves 6 as a side dish

Method:

1. Mix all the dressing ingredients together and season to taste. I like a tart dressing, so I use lots of vinegar and mustard. Add more olive oil if it's too tart. Leave the dressing to infuse.
2. Boil or steam the potatoes for 15 minutes, until just tender. Drain very well in a colander, then transfer to a bowl and pour over the mustard dressing. Remove the garlic clove.
3. Crisp up the bacon on the grill, then cut into small pieces (but not too small). Drain on kitchen paper to remove any excess fat.
4. Boil the eggs for 7 minutes, until hard-boiled but not overdone. Drain and pour over cold water, then peel and halve.
5. Mix two-thirds of the bacon, eggs, pickles, spring onions and parsley through the hot potatoes. Garnish with the rest. This is delicious served hot or cold.

Wholegrain mustard, also called granary mustard, is an indispensable Pantry Pal for making salad dressings, sauces and marinades. Just a smidgen adds tons of flavour. The yellow and black mustard seeds are left whole, and even though it's peppery and tart, it's quite mild in comparison to a hot English mustard. Use in cooking or as a condiment on cold meats and sandwiches.

Spicy Chakalaka Bean Salad

Ingredients:

- 1 tbsp sunflower oil
- 2 red peppers, sliced
- 1 green pepper, sliced
- 1 large red onion, sliced
- 1 head of cauliflower, broken into florets
- 2 lemons
- 1 tbsp light brown sugar
- 1 tbsp strong curry powder
- 5 large tomatoes, roughly chopped
- 1 x 400g tin of cannellini beans, rinsed and drained
- 1 carrot, grated
- salt and freshly ground black pepper
- 4 tbsp chopped fresh coriander

Serves 6 as a side dish or condiment

Method:

1. Heat the oil in a large frying pan over a medium heat. Cook the peppers and onion for about 15 minutes, until soft.
2. Steam the cauliflower florets for 3 minutes, until they're just tender but still have a bite. Refresh under cold water and leave in a colander to drain. Squeeze over the juice of 1 lemon and coat well with the juice.
3. Add the sugar and curry powder to the peppers and onion. Stir well to dissolve the sugar. Add the chopped tomatoes and simmer on a low heat for 15 minutes, until the tomatoes are pulpy and saucy. Mix through the beans, grated carrot and cauliflower. Taste and season well with the juice of the remaining lemon and some salt and pepper.
4. Transfer to a large bowl and allow to cool completely before stirring in the fresh coriander.

Curry powder in the South African pantry is essential. We have a large Indian population – in fact, most of the province of Natal is of Indian origin. The curry powder commonly found in supermarkets is a generic blend of spices that was developed for Western tastes and comes in mild, medium and hot versions. In proper Indian cooking there are a vast array of spice blends, but this is a good stand-by.

Ouma Polly's Green Fig Preserve

Ingredients:

- 1 tbsp bread soda
- 2.5 litres water
- 1kg ripe, firm figs
- 1.2kg granulated sugar
- 1 cinnamon stick
- 3 tbsp lemon juice

Makes 2 x 500ml Kilner jars

Method:

1. Dissolve the bread soda in the water. Add the figs and soak them overnight. This softens the fruit but keeps the skin firm. The next day, drain and rinse them very well.
2. Remove the rubber seal from two 500ml glass jars and wash the jars in hot soapy water. Rinse very well in clean water and place upside on the oven shelf. Bake for 10 minutes at 150°C to dry and sterilise the jars.
3. Fill a large pot with water and add the figs. Boil for 15 minutes, until tender. Drain in a colander.
4. Fill the pot with 2 litres of fresh water. Add the sugar, cinnamon stick and lemon juice. Bring to the boil, stirring, until the sugar dissolves.
5. Carefully drop in the figs and cook for about 45 minutes, until the figs are translucent and the syrup has thickened.
6. Bottle the hot figs and their syrup immediately in the warm, sterilised jars, sealing tightly. Store in a cool, dark place for up to 6 months.
7. Serve with bread, lamb and cheese boards.

Cinnamon sticks are the real workhorses of the kitchen. They're essential in desserts such as fruit compotes and apple pies, but are equally important in savoury meaty dishes like tagines and curries. Sri Lankan cinnamon is the mostly highly prized for the best flavour. Keep cinnamon sticks and ground cinnamon for all your recipe needs.

Monica's Amarula Malva Pudding with Vanilla Clementine Syrup

Ingredients:

Malva sponge:
- 250ml caster sugar
- 2 tbsp butter, softened
- 1 tbsp apricot jam
- 2 eggs
- 125ml milk
- 1 tsp vinegar
- 1 tsp bread soda
- 250ml plain flour

Amarula caramel sauce:
- 125g butter
- 200ml cream
- 180ml sugar
- 125ml boiling water
- 6 tbsp Amarula liqueur
- 1 tsp vanilla essence

Vanilla clementine syrup:
- 250ml (1 cup) sugar
- 250ml (1 cup) water
- 1 vanilla bean, halved and seeds scraped out, or 2 tsp vanilla bean paste
- 8 whole clementines, peeled
- 1 cinnamon stick

- vanilla ice cream, to serve

Serves 8

Method:

Use a measuring jug to measure the dry ingredients – they are measured by volume, not weight.

1. To make the malva sponge, preheat the oven to 180°C. Grease a lasagne-type oven dish.
2. Cream the sugar, butter and apricot jam together. Add the eggs one at a time and beat until light and fluffy.
3. Mix the milk, vinegar and bread soda together in a separate small bowl and stir well. Gradually add the flour to the butter and sugar mixture, alternating with the milk, until completely mixed. Pour the batter into the oven dish and bake for 45 minutes. Alternatively, you can bake the sponge in 8 individual pots or ramekins for 20 minutes.
4. Meanwhile, to make the Amarula sauce, place all the sauce ingredients in a pot and melt together. Bring it just to the boil, then reduce to a simmer until the pudding is done. When the pudding comes out of the oven, poke holes in it and pour over the hot sauce, allowing it to sink in.
5. To make the vanilla clementine syrup, combine the sugar, water and vanilla bean seeds or paste in a pot. Gently bring to the boil and do not stir. Allow the syrup to bubble up and thicken for 5 minutes. Drag a spoon through the bottom, like Moses parting the Red Sea – the spoon should leave a clear path behind it before the gap closes. Add the whole clementines and cinnamon stick and poach for 5 minutes.
6. Serve the malva pudding warm with the vanilla clementines and ice cream.

Amarula is a South African cream liqueur made with fermented amarula fruit and cream. It has a wonderful caramel-like flavour and creamy richness that's ideal simply served as a drink on crushed ice. Or add it to you custard mix for a bread and butter pudding, in panna cotta or simply mixed with whipped cream for a meringue roulade.

Aloe Vera Cucumber Punch

Ingredients:

- 2 bottles chenic blanc, well chilled
- 250ml white rum
- 250ml aloe vera juice
- 1 cucumber, peeled into ribbons
- Large handful of fresh mint
- 1 litre sparkling water or soda water, well chilled
- ice cubes, to serve
- extra fresh mint sprigs, to serve

Serves 15

Method:

1. Mix together the white wine, rum and aloe vera juice.
2. In a large glass jug, add the cucumber and fresh mint. Fill the jug with the punch.
3. For each glass, add 4 to 5 ice cubes, and fill two thirds of the way with punch. Top up with sparkling water or soda water and a sprig of fresh mint.

Rooibos Pomegranate Iced Tea

Ingredients:

- 4 rooibos tea bags, or 4tbsp loose tea
- 1/2 cup of honey
- 1 litre of boiling water
- 1 litre of pomegranate juice, well chilled
- 250ml orange juice
- seeds of 1/2 pomegranate
- 2 lemons, sliced, to serve
- ice cubes, to serve

Serves 15

Method:

1. Add the boiling water to the tea and honey. Allow to steep for 7 minutes.
2. Remove the tea bags or strain if using loose tea.
3. Pour the chilled pomegranate and orange juice into the rooibos tea, add the pomegranate seeds, allow to cool then place in the fridge to cool further.
4. Fill each glass with 4 to 5 ice cubes and 2 to 3 slices of lemon. Serve the rooibos pomegranate iced tea from a large jug.

Chapter 2

Irish

Black Pudding Burgers

Ingredients:

- 500g steak mince
- 280g black pudding
- 1 small red onion, finely diced
- burger buns, to serve

Makes 4 burgers

Method:

1. Mix the mince, black pudding and diced onion together with clean, wet hands, but don't overhandle. Shape into 4 firm, round burger patties. Cover and chill in the fridge for 1 hour to firm up.
2. Cook under the grill, on a pan or ideally a BBQ. Cook evenly on both sides for 8–10 minutes, until cooked through.
3. Serve in a lightly toasted bun with a topping of your choice.

My favourite toppings for Black Pudding Burgers:

1. Bacon, avocado and blue cheese: Add crispy rashers, slices of ripe avocado and Cashel Blue cheese.
2. Pickled cucumber: Thinly slice 1 large cucumber and place in a heatproof bowl. Put 125ml (1/2 cup) white wine vinegar, 1 clove of peeled garlic, 1 bay leaf, 2 tablespoons fresh chopped dill, 2 teaspoons sugar, 1 teaspoon salt and 1 teaspoon mustard seeds in a small pot and bring to the boil. Pour the pickling mixture over the cucumbers, allow to cool and serve.
3. Pickled or roasted beetroot: Grate fresh, peeled, raw beetroot into a bowl. Cover generously with balsamic vinegar and season with salt and pepper. Add a few fresh rosemary sprigs and allow to 'pickle' for 20 minutes.
4. Blue cheese mayonnaise: Mash together 1 clove of crushed garlic, 4 tablespoons mayonnaise, 1 tablespoon blue cheese and freshly ground black pepper.
5. Horseradish crème fraîche: Mix 4 tablespoons crème fraîche with 1 clove of crushed garlic, 1 tablespoon horseradish sauce, a good squeeze of lemon juice and some salt and freshly ground black pepper.

Versions of black pudding appear in several different cuisines, not just Ireland's. Black pudding is often served as a breakfast item, but it's equally delicious served with scallops, in warm salads and as a stuffing. I favour traditional artisan producers and unique recipes like smoked black pudding.

Crispy Pork Belly

Ingredients:

- 1kg pork belly, skin removed
- 2 fennel bulbs, very finely sliced
- juice of 1 lemon
- rapeseed oil
- 4 pears, cored and quartered lengthways (skin on)
- 4 apples, cut into thick rings (skin on)
- salt and freshly ground black pepper
- 150g baby salad leaves
- 1/2 pomegranate, seeds only

Marinade:
- 170g (1 cup) dark brown sugar
- 1 litre apple juice
- 125ml (1/2 cup) apple cider vinegar
- 125ml (1/2 cup) soy sauce
- 3 cloves of garlic, finely chopped
- freshly ground black pepper
- 4 sprigs of fresh rosemary
- 4 sprigs of fresh thyme

Serves 8

Method:

1. Preheat the oven to 160°C.
2. Cut the pork belly into large cubes and thread onto bamboo skewers, with the fatty side facing outward. Place the skewers in a close-fitting ovenproof dish.
3. To make the marinade, gently heat the sugar, apple juice, apple cider vinegar and soy sauce together. Add the garlic and season with black pepper. Pour the liquid over the skewers and tuck in the rosemary and thyme sprigs.
4. Cover the dish with foil and cook for 30 minutes. Discard the foil, raise the heat to 180°C and continue to cook for 30 minutes more.
5. While the kebabs are cooking, place the fennel slices in a bowl and cover with the lemon juice.
6. Remove the kebabs from the oven and grill on a hot BBQ until they crisp up, basting continuously with the sauce from the dish.
7. Lightly oil the pears and apples and season with salt and pepper. Grill on a medium-hot BBQ until the fruit is charred and slightly softened.
8. Skim the fat from the sauce and discard. Place the remaining sauce in a small pot and boil until reduced down to a thick syrup.
9. Serve the pork skewers on a bed of baby salad leaves along with the grilled pears and apples, lemony fennel slices, a scattering of pomegranate seeds and a drizzle of the reduced sauce.

Apple cider vinegar is an essential Pantry Pal for salad dressings, marinades and to make homemade chutneys and pickles. Mild and sweet, it's a fail-safe choice when in doubt. Try an organic brand for extra apple intensity.

Biscuit Tin Hot Smoked Salmon

Ingredients:

- 400g salmon fillet
- 1 tsp salt
- 1 tsp caster sugar
- 1/2 cup of embers (almost burnt-out coals)
- 2 Rooibosch teabags or 2 tbsp loose tea

Makes 400g

Method:

1. Rub the salmon with the salt and sugar. Wrap well in cling film and cure in the fridge overnight. The next day, rinse the salmon well and pat it dry.
2. Place the embers in an old biscuit tin with the teabags. Light the teabags or loose tea and place a wire rack on top. Put the salmon on the wire rack. Close the lid on the biscuit tin and leave for 20 minutes.
3. Remove the salmon and enjoy it hot or cold.

Rooibosch tea is a naturally caffeine-free tea native to South Africa. Fragrant and aromatic, it's delicious as an herbal tea but also to stew dried fruit in, as a marinade for pork and to flavour desserts like panna cotta. Try it with honey and lemon, or even milk and sugar, like a Ceylon tea.

Angela's Beetroot Superfood Salad

Ingredients:

- 4 fresh beetroot
- 4 tbsp balsamic vinegar
- 2 tbsp olive oil
- salt and freshly ground black pepper
- 150g watercress
- 100g goat cheese, roughly broken into pieces
- 100g alfalfa shoots
- 50g sunflower seeds
- 1/2 pomegranate, seeds only
- 2 tbsp finely chopped fresh dill

Serves 4

Method:

1. Preheat the oven to 180°C.
2. Peel and dice the beetroot into bite-size pieces. Coat well in the balsamic vinegar and olive oil and season with salt and pepper. Place on a baking tray and roast in the oven for 20–30 minutes, until just tender. Allow to cool slightly.
3. Divide the watercress between 4 plates and place the cooled beetroot on top. Scatter over the goat cheese, alfalfa shoots, sunflower seeds, pomegranate seeds and dill.
4. Drizzle over the roasting juices from the baking tray and a little extra olive oil and balsamic vinegar if desired.

Alfalfa shoots are one of the many seeds that can be sprouted to produce delicate, crunchy green fronds that add terrific nutrition, texture and crunch to salads, wraps, sandwiches and stir-frys. These are very easy to sprout yourself, but most supermarkets sell tubs of them in the salad section.

Spring Vegetable Potato Salad

Ingredients:

- 500g baby potatoes, halved
- 250g baby carrots, scrubbed clean
- 250g green beans, trimmed and cut into thirds
- 1 x 400g tin of chickpeas, drained and rinsed
- 1 small jar of artichoke hearts in oil, drained
- 4 tbsp chopped fresh flat-leaf parsley
- 1 tsp pink peppercorns, crushed

Dressing:
- 1 clove of garlic, crushed
- juice of 1/2 lemon
- 3 tbsp Greek yoghurt
- 3 tbsp crème fraîche or sour cream
- 1 tsp Dijon mustard
- salt and freshly ground black pepper

Serves 8

Method:

1. Mix all the dressing ingredients together and season to taste. You may use more lemon juice if you prefer.
2. Steam the potatoes for 12–15 minutes, until just tender. Allow to cool in a colander.
3. Steam the carrots for 4–5 minutes, until just tender. You can halve them if they're on the big side.
4. Steam the green beans for 3 minutes, then plunge into ice water to refresh them.
5. Put the cooked veggies, chickpeas and artichoke hearts in a bowl and mix the dressing through.
6. Garnish with fresh chopped parsley and crushed pink peppercorns.

Dijon mustard is an indispensable Pantry Pal. It's my go to condiment for salad dressings, both creamy and oil based. It really lifts a creamy dressing and dispenses with the need for mayonnaise. Dijon is savoury and flavoursome, but subtle enough to mellow other flavours.

Herby Tartare Homemade Ricotta with Smoked Salmon

Ingredients:

- 1 litre full-fat milk
- 500ml cream
- 1 tsp sea salt
- 3 tbsp white wine vinegar
- 1/2 red onion, finely chopped
- 2 tbsp chopped fresh dill
- 2 tbsp finely chopped fresh chives
- 1 tbsp small capers
- juice of 1/2 lemon
- salt and freshly ground black pepper

Serve with:
- Irish brown soda bread
- smoked salmon
- lemon wedges
- dill fronds

Makes 1 bowl

Method:

1. Mix the milk, cream and salt in a large pot. Bring to the boil, stirring to dissolve the salt. Turn off the heat and stir in the vinegar. The mixture will go lumpy and will curdle.
2. Line a large colander or sieve with 2 layers of muslin. Stand this over a large bowl. Pour the curdled milk into the colander. Allow to stand for 1 hour. Discard the liquid that collects in the bowl.
3. You'll be left with thick, creamy ricotta cheese that's ready to use as is or seasoned. Add the red onion, dill, chives, capers, lemon juice and some salt and pepper. Cover and refrigerate for up to 4 days.
4. This is delicious served on toasted rustic bread with smoked salmon.

Smoked salmon is so quintessentially Irish. When I first moved here I lived on brown soda bread and smoked salmon for the first few weeks. It will shock the puritans, but I do freeze packs of smoked salmon so that I always have some. My favourite light meal is a poached egg, steamed asparagus and smoked salmon.

Grilled Caraway Cabbage

Ingredients:

- 1 head of red cabbage
- 50ml (1/4 cup) rapeseed oil
- salt and freshly ground black pepper
- 4 tbsp chopped fresh flat-leaf parsley

Dressing:
- 125ml (1/2 cup) apple cider vinegar
- 50ml (1/4 cup) rapeseed oil
- 1 tsp sugar
- 1 tsp caraway seeds
- 1/2 tsp salt
- 1/2 tsp freshly ground black pepper

Serves 8

Method:

1. Remove the loosest, toughest outer leaves from the cabbage and discard them. Cut the cabbage into 8 evenly sized wedges. Do not remove the stalk or inner core, as this is holding the wedges together.
2. Brush the cabbage with the rapeseed oil and season well with salt and pepper. Place the wedges on the grill and cook for 5–7 minutes on each of the 3 sides of the wedges, until the edges have blackened and the inner leaves have softened. Move the cabbage to a cooler part of the BBQ until it's cooked to your liking. Insert a dinner knife to see how firm it is inside. Remove the cabbage when it's beginning to wilt but is still a bit firm in the middle.
3. To make the dressing, mix the apple cider vinegar, rapeseed oil, sugar, caraway seeds, salt and pepper together and dress the cabbage well. Garnish with fresh chopped parsley.

Rapeseed grows extremely well in Ireland and produces a golden, nutty oil that's perfect for sautéing, grilling and salad dressings. It's a great alternative to olive oil when you're looking for a different flavour to suit a certain dish.

Pots of Gold

Ingredients:

- 1 loaf of rustic bread (such as sourdough), sliced
- 2 tbsp rapeseed oil
- 2 bunches of red seedless grapes
- 4 small wheels of Brie or Camembert-style cheeses

Serves 4

Method:

1. Toast the bread slices on a medium grill or BBQ until charred with grill marks. Keep warm.
2. Lightly oil the bunches of grapes and place the whole bunches on a medium-hot grill until they start to burst.
3. Place the cheeses on a medium-hot grill until they're charred and starting to melt.
4. Serve the grilled cheese hot with the grapes and toasted bread.

I have a great love of cheese and one of my favourite jobs was judging the Irish Cheese Awards – not really work at all! With such a selection of excellent cheeses to choose from, it's worthwhile spending some time trying samples at cheese counters and delicatessens.

Margaret's Best Brown Bread

Ingredients:

- 400g coarse stone-ground brown flour
- 100g plain flour
- 50g seeds (pumpkin, sunflower, sesame, chia, poppy, flaxseed), plus extra for sprinkling
- 50g porridge oat flakes, plus extra for sprinkling
- 1 level tsp bread soda
- 1 tsp salt
- 450ml buttermilk
- 2 tbsp sunflower oil
- 1 tbsp treacle or molasses

Makes 1 loaf

Method:

1. Preheat the oven to 200°C. Line a baking tray with parchment paper or dust with extra flour.
2. Place the dry ingredients in a large bowl and mix thoroughly. Make a well in the centre.
3. Mix the buttermilk, oil and treacle in a jug. Pour the liquid into the well of the dry ingredients. Mix with a wooden spoon or your hands to form a sloppy, wet dough.
4. Pour the dough onto the prepared tray and shape into a round. Score a cross in the loaf and sprinkle over some seeds and oat flakes.
5. Bake for 35–40 minutes. When you tap the bottom of the loaf, it should sound hollow. For a more even crust, I often turn the loaf over for the last 10 minutes. If the crust is very hard, wrap the bread in a clean, wet tea towel to soften it.
6. Allow to cool on a wire rack before slicing.

Stone-ground brown flour is essential to making good brown bread. Difficult to find outside Ireland, coarsely ground brown flour using traditional milling methods produces a nutty bread with a lovely texture. If your flour is particularly fibrous, you may need to add more buttermilk to achieve a wet dough typical of a soda bread.

Crunchy Courgette Pickle

Ingredients:

- 500g courgettes
- 3 shallots, finely sliced
- pinch of salt
- 140g caster sugar
- 500ml apple cider vinegar
- 3 tbsp sea salt
- 1 tsp English mustard powder
- 1 tsp turmeric
- 1 tsp mustard seeds
- 1 tsp celery seeds
- 1/2 tsp dried chilli flakes

Makes 1 litre

Method:

1. If you collect used glass jars for preserving, make sure the lids fit securely and haven't been bashed or dinged. If any air gets into the pickle, it will contaminate it.
2. Give the jars and lids a good wash in hot soapy water and rinse well. Try to get any labels off the jars. Boiling the bottles in a large pot of water is very effective too. Heat an oven to 150°C and dry the clean bottles and lids in the oven for 10–15 minutes.
3. Thinly slice the courgettes using a sharp knife, mandoline or the slicing blade of a food processor. Put in a colander with the shallots and a pinch of salt between the layers of vegetables. Leave for 1 hour to draw out the water. Rinse well and pat dry with kitchen paper.
4. Meanwhile, place the remaining ingredients into a large pan and bring to a simmer. Bubble for 3 minutes, making sure that the sugar has dissolved. Switch off the heat and leave to cool for 5 minutes, then add the courgettes and shallots.
5. Bottle the courgette pickle immediately in the clean, sterilised jars. Seal well, then allow to cool and refrigerate. The pickle will stay fresh for 2 months if chilled.

Celery seeds might seem like an odd ish factor, but they're very useful as a Pantry Pal. Celery seeds have a natural savoury, salty flavour, so grind them down with sea salt to produce a healthy, low-salt seasoning. They're also delish in a not-so-healthy bloody Mary!

Monica's Berry Baileys Meringue Roulade

Ingredients:

Meringue base:
- 5 egg whites
- 250g caster sugar

Baileys cream filling:
- 500ml cream, lightly whipped
- 4 tbsp Baileys Irish cream liqueur
- 1 tbsp icing sugar

Berry filling:
- 1 punnet of strawberries, halved
- 1 punnet of raspberries
- 1 punnet of blueberries
- 1 punnet of blackberries
- 1 punnet of Cape gooseberries

- 1 slab of white chocolate, to make chocolate curls
- icing sugar, to decorate

Serves 6

Method:

1. Preheat the oven to 150°C. Place a sheet of parchment paper on a baking tray. The paper must overhang the tray so that you can lift it out. You can stick the paper to the tray with sunflower oil. Lightly oil the top of the paper too to make it non-stick.
2. To make the meringue base, whisk the egg whites in a very clean, dry bowl until stiff peaks form. Gradually snow in the caster sugar and continue to whisk until the sugar dissolves – this is key. Rub the mixture between your fingers – if it feels sandy, carry on whisking.
3. Spread the meringue mixture evenly over the paper. Bake for 25 minutes, until the meringue is crunchy on top. It will still be marshmallowy underneath.
4. Gently lift the meringue off the baking tray using the paper and allow to cool on a wire rack. Once it's cool, place another piece of paper on top, grip firmly and turn the meringue over. Peel the top layer of parchment paper away.
5. To make the filling, whip together the cream, Baileys and icing sugar. Set aside.
6. Make the chocolate curls by 'shaving' the smooth side of the slab of chocolate with a vegetable peeler to scrape off a layer of chocolate that will curl. Set aside.
7. Lay the meringue with the longest side going from west to east. Make a gentle incision across 10cm from closest to you. Spread most of the whipped cream over the meringue base.
8. Scatter evenly with strawberries, raspberries, blueberries, blackberries and gooseberries. Using the paper, lift the edge of the meringue and roll it over into a log.
9. Scatter over the rest of the berries. Decorate with the rest of the cream, a sprinkling of white chocolate curls and a dusting of icing sugar.

Baileys and other Irish cream liqueurs aren't just for Christmas. They're delicious in after dinner coffee, simply drizzled over ice cream or added to recipes like cheesecake to add something special. I even add a good glug to my bread and butter pudding with white chocolate and cherries. Delish!

Irish Cream Boozy Milkshake

Ingredients:

- 1 bottle squeezy chocolate sauce
- 50ml whiskey
- 2 tsp dark crème de cacao
- 2 tsp Bailey's
- 100 milk
- 50ml cream
- 2 scoops vanilla ice cream

Serves 1

Method:

1. Put all the ingredients in a blender and blend until smooth.
2. Take a very chilled glass and squeeze a little chocolate sauce down the sides and swirl it.
3. Pour the milkshake into the glass and serve with a straw.

Apple and Sage Irish Breakfast Iced Tea

Ingredients:

- 4 Irish Breakfast Tea teabags, or 4 tbsp of loose tea
- 1 litre boiling water
- 1 litre apple juice, well chilled
- juice of 1/2 lemon
- 8 sprigs of sage leaves
- ice cubes, to serve

Serves 8

Method:

1. Add the boiling water to the tea. Allow to steep for 7 minutes.
2. Remove the tea bags or strain if using loose tea.
3. Pour the chilled apple and lemon juice into the tea, allow to cool then place in the fridge to cool further.
4. Serve with ice and a sprig of fresh sage.

Chapter 3

Thai*ish*

Thai-spiced Ostrich Fillet Steak with Mango Salad

Ingredients:

- 4 thick ostrich fillet steaks
  (you can also use beef fillet)

Marinade:
- 3 cloves of garlic, crushed
- 3 tbsp hoisin sauce
- 2 tbsp fish sauce
- 1 1/2 tbsp paprika
- 1 tbsp soy sauce
- 1 tbsp sunflower oil
- 2 tsp dried oregano
- 1 tsp ground thyme
- 1 tsp cayenne pepper
- 1/2 tsp ground black pepper
- 1/2 tsp ground white pepper

Salad:
- 2 mangoes, sliced into long strips
- 1 red onion, thinly sliced into
  half moons
- 250g cherry tomatoes, halved
- 150g baby salad leaves
- 100g micro salad leaves/mixed
  sprouts, plus extra to garnish
- 2 tbsp chopped fresh coriander,
  plus extra to garnish

Dressing:
- 2 cloves of garlic, crushed
- 1 red chilli, finely sliced, plus extra
  to garnish
- juice of 1 lime
- 1 tbsp soy sauce
- 1 tbsp fish sauce
- 1 tsp palm sugar or caster sugar
- 1 tsp rice wine vinegar
- pinch of white pepper

Serves 6

Method:

1. Mix all the marinade ingredients together. Keep aside 2 tablespoons of marinade to baste with.
2. Coat the ostrich fillets in the marinade, cover and marinade for 1–4 hours.
3. Place the steaks on a hot BBQ and seal for 3 minutes a side. This will give you a rare to medium-rare steak, depending on the thickness of the steak. Baste the steak well. If you prefer your steak medium to well done, move it to a cooler part of the BBQ and cook through. This recipe works best with a medium-rare steak.
4. Remove the steak from the BBQ when it's cooked to your liking. Loosely cover with foil on a warm plate and allow to rest for 5 minutes.
5. Divide the salad ingredients between 4 plates and arrange artistically. Slice the steak and scatter it over the salad.
6. Mix all the dressing ingredients together and drizzle over the salad. Garnish with extra sprouts, chillies and coriander.

Fish sauce (nam pla) is the salt of South-East Asia and is an essential Pantry Pal for this chapter. Even though it's made from fermented fish and salt, the fishiness disappears once it's mixed with lime juice – I promise! Used in every Thai curry, sauce and salad dressing, fish sauce is vital to balance flavours and get that authentic taste. Once opened, store it in the fridge.

BBQ Prawn, Avocado and Melon Salad

Ingredients:

- 24 large tiger prawns, peeled, headed and deveined
- 2 ripe avocados, sliced
- 1/2 red onion, finely sliced into half moons
- 250g watermelon balls (use a melon baller)
- 250g green melon balls (use a melon baller)
- 250g spanspek (cantaloupe) melon balls (use a melon baller)
- 250g baby yellow tomatoes, halved
- 100g alfalfa and radish shoots
- large handful of mint

Marinade:
- 2 cloves of garlic, crushed
- 1 thumb-sized piece of fresh ginger, finely grated
- juice of 4 limes
- 1 tbsp sweet chilli sauce
- 1 tbsp kecap manis (Indonesian soy sauce)

Dressing:
- 1 red chilli, very finely chopped
- juice of 4 limes
- 1 tbsp fish sauce
- 1 tbsp caster sugar
- 1 tsp grated lemongrass

Serves 4 as a main or 6 as a starter

Method:

1. Mix all the dressing ingredients together and leave to infuse.
2. Mix all the marinade ingredients together, then pour it over the prawns and set aside for 20 minutes. Grill the prawns on a hot BBQ until they're firm, pink and curled, with definite griddle marks – they only take a few minutes.
3. Gently mix the avocados, onion, melons and tomatoes. Add the prawns and work through gently. Drizzle over the dressing, going easy over the watermelon, as it sucks up dressing.
4. Garnish with the alfalfa and radish shoots and fresh mint. Serve warm or cold, either from one big platter or divided amongst plates.

Kecap manis is a thick, sweet dark soy sauce from Indonesia. It has the pouring consistency of maple syrup so is ideal for marinades and bastes. You can mix it with other sauces and ingredients to cook with or make a dressing, and it is ideal as a condiment for stir-fries, noodle dishes and rice dishes like nasi goreng. Invest in a large bottle from the Asian market-it has a good shelf life.

Chicken Skewers with Peanut Pesto

Ingredients:

- 4 chicken breasts, cut into bite-sized cubes
- 1 tbsp sesame seeds, toasted

Marinade:
- 1 clove of garlic, crushed
- 150ml soy sauce
- 1 tbsp grated fresh ginger
- 1 tbsp toasted sesame oil
- 1 tbsp sunflower oil

Peanut pesto:
- 300ml coconut milk
- 500g roasted, salted peanuts
- 4 cloves of garlic
- 3 green chillies
- 3 lime leaves
- 2 stalks of lemongrass, white part only
- 1/2 red onion
- juice of 2 limes
- 1 tbsp light brown sugar
- 1 tbsp fish sauce
- 30g (1 cup) fresh basil leaves
- 15g (1/2 cup) fresh coriander leaves
- 15g (1/2 cup) fresh mint leaves

Serves 8

Method:

1. Soak 16 bamboo skewers in cold water for 1 hour to prevent charring.
2. Mix all the marinade ingredients together and pour it over the chicken. Leave to marinate for 1 hour, then thread the chicken onto the skewers.
3. On a hot BBQ, grill the chicken skewers for 15–20 minutes, until well browned with nice grill marks. Cut through the fattest piece to check that they're cooked through. Do not overcook, as chicken breasts can dry out very quickly.
4. To make the peanut pesto, pour the coconut milk into a food processor. Add all the pesto ingredients except the fresh herbs and pulse until a rough paste forms. Just before serving, add the fresh herbs and pulse again to form a rough pesto.
5. Serve the grilled chicken skewers sprinkled with toasted sesame seeds and drizzled with peanut pesto. Serve extra peanut pesto on the side.

Coconut milk is a staple in Thai cooking, used in curries, soups and salad dressings. I prefer thick, creamy coconut milk rather than the low-fat versions, as it makes a nicer sauce. Stock up on tins of coconut milk in Asian markets and beware of brands where starch or gluten are used as thickeners.

Thai Red Curry Mussels in Foil

Ingredients:

- 1 tbsp Thai red curry paste
- 1 x 400g tin of coconut milk
- 1 stalk of lemongrass, divided into 4 chunks and bruised
- juice of 2 limes
- 1 tbsp palm sugar or light brown sugar
- 1 tbsp fish sauce
- 1.5kg fresh mussels, scrubbed clean and beards removed

To serve:
- 6 spring onions, sliced
- 2 tomatoes, peeled and diced concasse
- 2 red chillies, finely sliced
- large bunch of fresh coriander, chopped
- 4 limes, cut into wedges
- cooked basmati rice

Serves 4

Method:

1. Heat the Thai red curry paste in a small saucepan with a little of the coconut milk. When it's fragrant, add the rest of the coconut milk and the lemongrass, lime juice, palm sugar and fish sauce and melt together.
2. Tear off 8 large squares of heavy-duty aluminium foil. Double up layers of foil to form 4 parcels. If any mussels are open, tap them on the worktop and discard them if they don't close. Divide the mussels between the 4 parcels and pile them up in the middle of each foil parcel. Pour the sauce over each parcel and crimp together tightly until well sealed.
3. Place the foil parcel directly on the BBQ or on an enamel dish first. Cook for 10–15 minutes, until the mussels open – it takes a little longer than on the hob, depending on the heat of the BBQ. If any mussels haven't opened at this point, discard them.
4. Open the parcels and garnish with spring onions, tomatoes, sliced red chillies and plenty of coriander. Serve with extra lime wedges and a small bowl of basmati rice.

Thai red curry paste is one of several curry pastes used in Thai cooking, each with its own unique flavour and ingredients. Curry paste has a wet consistency and is used as a base for curry sauces. Readily available, it's also easy to make your own. Typical ingredients include red chillies, shallots, garlic, galangal, lemongrass, lime, coriander, cumin seeds, peppercorns and shrimp paste. Thai red curry paste goes well with chicken, prawns, beef, white fish and duck.

Whole Baked Fish in Banana Leaves

Ingredients:

- 1 whole large fish or 4 small ones (such as snoek, sea bass, salmon, mackerel), cleaned, scaled and gutted
- 2 oranges, unpeeled and sliced
- 2 red onions, sliced
- 1 large banana leaf
- lime wedges, to serve
- red chilli slices, to garnish

Filling:
- 3 cloves of garlic, crushed
- 1 orange, unpeeled and sliced
- 1 red onion, sliced
- 1 red chilli, sliced
- 1 thumb-sized piece of fresh galangal, julienned
- 1 stalk of lemongrass, grated (use a Microplane grater)
- 100ml soy sauce
- 100ml sunflower oil
- 2 tbsp honey

Serves 4

Method:

1. Score diagonal lines on the skin on both sides of the fish. Layer half the orange and onion slices on the banana leaf, then put the fish on top.
2. Mix all the filling ingredients together, then spoon the filling into the cavity of the fish. Cover the fish with another layer of orange and onion slices. Wrap the fish in the banana leaf and secure with string.
3. Place on a medium-hot BBQ and cover with the lid of the BBQ or a metal dish. Grill until the fish is flaky and cooked through. This will vary depending on the size of the fish, but it should take approximately 35–40 minutes for a whole small fish like mackerel and up to 90 minutes for a whole salmon.
4. Serve in the banana leaf with lime wedges and extra chilli slices.

Galangal is an aromatic root that's widely used in Thai cooking, available fresh, dried and in powdered form from Asian markets. Try to use fresh galangal instead of dried. At a push, you can substitute fresh ginger for galangal, but they're different in taste and appearance. Galangal has a more peppery taste and a scent like fresh pine.

Crunchy Asian Coleslaw

Ingredients:

- 2 packets of instant 2-minute noodles
- 4 tbsp white sesame seeds
- 4 tbsp black sesame seeds
- 6 spring onions, sliced diagonally
- 2 medium carrots, peeled into ribbons
- 1 small green cabbage, very thinly sliced
- 1 small purple cabbage, very thinly sliced
- 1/2 Chinese cabbage, very finely sliced
- 1/2 cucumber, peeled into ribbons
- 2 tbsp chopped fresh mint
- 2 tbsp chopped fresh basil
- 2 tbsp chopped fresh coriander
- 50g roasted peanuts

Dressing:
- 125ml grapeseed oil
- 75ml rice wine vinegar
- 4 tbsp soy sauce
- 2 tbsp caster sugar

Serves 8 as a side dish

Method:

1. Mix together all the dressing ingredients and set aside.
2. Break the noodles into pieces and toast in a clean, dry pan. Alternatively, fry them in a little sunflower oil until puffed up and crispy.
3. Toast the sesame seeds in a clean, dry pan until lightly toasted and starting to pop.
4. Toss together the spring onions, carrots, cabbages, cucumber and fresh herbs. Garnish with the crispy noodles, toasted sesame seeds and peanuts.
5. Just before serving, mix through the dressing.

Rice wine vinegar and rice vinegar are the same thing. Rice wine is an alcohol made from fermenting the sugars in rice to form alcohol. To make vinegar, this fermentation process is taken one step further. Rice wine vinegars are produced across Asia and vary quite dramatically. In general, rice vinegar is far less acidic than Western vinegars, so it's preferable not to substitute. Rice wine vinegar is widely used in salad dressings, dipping sauces and marinades.

Fruity Floral Crispy Noodle Salad

Ingredients:

- 50g instant 2-minute noodles
- 1 head of butter lettuce
- 1 papaya
- 1 large avocado
- juice of 1 lime
- 150g strawberries
- large bunch of basil leaves
- edible flowers, to garnish

Dressing:
- 6 tbsp avocado oil
- 3 tbsp raspberry vinegar
- salt and freshly ground black pepper

Serves 4

Method:

1. Toast the noodles in a clean, dry pan until crispy. Alternatively, shallow fry them in a little sunflower oil until puffed up and crispy.
2. Mix all the dressing ingredients together and season with salt and pepper. I like a tart dressing, so I use a little more vinegar.
3. Wash the lettuce leaves and break into bite-sized pieces. Peel the papaya into long strips with a sharp vegetable peeler. Slice the avocado into long strips and coat with the lime juice. Slice the strawberries lengthways.
4. Gently mix the salad ingredients together and arrange on a platter. Scatter over the crispy noodles, basil leaves and edible flowers. Drizzle with a little dressing and serve immediately.

Edible flowers are one of my favourite garnishes for spring and summer salads. Some plants have leaves, fruit and flowers that are edible, such as rocket, chives and courgettes. For really colourful edible flowers, plant borage, black velvet nasturtiums, violas, princess of India nasturtiums and marigolds. They're easy to grow in pots and are a great foodie project.

Thai Rice Salad with Spiced Pineapple

Ingredients:

- 200g (1 cup) jasmine or basmati rice, cooked and allowed to cool
- 1/2 fresh pineapple, cut into long, chunky pieces
- juice of 1 lime
- 1 tsp chilli flakes
- 1 tsp ground cumin
- 1 tsp ground coriander
- 1 tsp sea salt
- large bunch of fresh coriander, roughly chopped
- 2 tbsp desiccated coconut, lightly toasted

Dressing:
- 2 fresh red chillies, sliced
- 1 thumb-sized piece of fresh ginger, grated
- 4 tbsp rice wine vinegar
- 1 tbsp caster sugar

Serves 6 as a side salad

Method:

1. Cook the rice according to the instructions below and allow to cool.
2. Mix all the dressing ingredients together and allow to infuse.
3. Add the pineapple, lime juice, spices and salt to a bowl. Allow to infuse for 10 minutes.
4. Grill the pineapple on a medium-hot BBQ for 8–10 minutes, until charred and softened. Once the pineapple is grilled, cut it into smaller dice and toss through the rice. Garnish with coriander and desiccated coconut.
5. Just before serving, pour the dressing over the salad.

Jasmine rice is native to Thailand and is a different species to basmati rice. It has a moist and sticky texture, rather than the fluffy, separate grains of basmati. To cook, combine 1 part well-rinsed rice and 2 parts water in a pot with a pinch of salt. Bring to the boil and boil for 5 minutes. Switch off the hob, clamp on a tight-fitting lid and leave covered for 30 minutes, then fluff up with a fork.

Green Bean, Coconut and Chilli Salad

Ingredients:

- 30g coconut shavings (available in Woolworths in the fridge section)
- 500g green beans, trimmed
- large bunch of fresh coriander, chopped

Dressing:
- 1 tbsp palm sugar or light brown sugar
- 1 tbsp sweet chilli sauce
- 1 tbsp rice wine vinegar
- zest and juice of 1 lime
- sea salt and freshly ground black pepper

Serves 6

Method:

1. Lightly toast the coconut shavings in a clean, dry pan and set aside.
2. Blanch the green beans in boiling water for 3 minutes, then plunge into ice water to refresh.
3. Mix all the dressing ingredients together until the sugar dissolves.
4. Drain the green beans well and drizzle with the dressing. Sprinkle over the toasted coconut and fresh coriander.

Palm sugar is made from the sap of several different palm trees. Widely used in Thai cooking, it's an essential Pantry Pal to balance the flavours of salty, bitter, sour and the heat from chillies. Buy it granulated in packets or in little cakes that you can grate. Palm sugar has a delicious caramel taste and adds depth of flavour, not just sweetness.

Homemade Sweet Chilli Sauce

Ingredients:

- 3 large red chillies, finely chopped
- 2 cloves of garlic, finely chopped
- 2 bay leaves
- 200g (1 cup) caster sugar
- 100ml white wine
- 100ml water
- 4 tbsp white wine vinegar
- 1 tbsp tomato paste
- 1 tsp salt
- 1 tsp ground white pepper

Makes 250ml

Method:

1. Place all the ingredients in a saucepan and heat gently, without stirring, until the sugar dissolves. Only stir the sauce once the sugar has dissolved and bring slowly up to the boil. Boil until syrupy and slightly thickened, then discard the bay leaves.
2. Wash a glass bottle in hot soapy water and dry it in the oven at 150°C for 10 minutes. As soon as the sauce is ready, use a funnel to pour the sauce into the sterilised bottle.

White pepper is widely used in South-East Asian cooking instead of black pepper. White pepper isn't as fruity or aromatic as black pepper and tends to have a sharper, more piquant taste. I think white pepper has a little more heat too. White pepper is also ideal for recipes and sauces, like a fresh mayonnaise, where black pepper would leave speckles and mar the appearance.

Hannah's Chocolatey Salted Peanut Brittle

Ingredients:

- 350g caster sugar
- 250g salted peanuts
- 75g butter
- 400g dark chocolate

Makes 1 large glass jar

Method:

1. Add the sugar to a stainless steel saucepan and place over a medium heat. Allow the sugar to melt and caramelise. Do not stir it, but rather, swirl the pot to mix the sugar around.
2. Line a baking tray with foil or a silicone mat. Lightly oil it and scatter over the peanuts.
3. When the sugar turns a golden colour, add the butter and remove it from the heat. Stir until the butter is melted and fully mixed in. Pour the caramel over the nuts, covering all of them. Allow to cool and harden.
4. Meanwhile, place a heatproof bowl over a pot of simmering water, making sure the water doesn't touch the bottom of the bowl. Break the chocolate into pieces and add to the bowl, stirring now and then until it's all melted.
5. Break the peanut brittle into large-ish chunks and dip half of each piece into the melted chocolate. Allow to set on a wire rack or a piece of parchment paper.
6. Store in a large glass jar or pretty biscuit tin or present the brittle in a gift box.

Using peanuts in cooking is more prevalent in Indonesia, and has been adopted into Thai cuisine with dishes like chicken satay and pad Thai noodles with peanuts. It's more authentic to use ground fresh peanuts to make these dishes, not peanut butter. I like the flavour of salted or roasted peanuts, so I tend to use these. Even a handful over a stir-fry or noodle dish makes it more interesting. Keep peanuts in the freezer to retain freshness and to stop you from eating them!

Pineapple Lime Tonic

Ingredients:

- 6 basil leaves
- 1 stick lemon grass, bruised
- 25ml gin
- 1 tsp lemon juice
- 1 tbsp lime cordial
- 100ml pineapple juice
- 50ml tonic water
- pineapple slices, to serve
- ice cubes, to serve

Serves 1

Method:

1. Crush the the basil with the lemongrass, gin, lemon juice, lime cordial, pineapple juice and tonic water.
2. Strain and serve over ice in a tall glass. Top up with extra tonic water.
3. Garnish with fresh pineapple.

Lemongrass Iced Tea

Ingredients:

- 3 stalks of fresh lemongrass
- 1 thumb of ginger, peeled and sliced
- 2 litres water
- 3 tbsp palm sugar or light brown sugar
- ice cubes, to serve

Serves 8

Method:

1. Bruise the lemongrass with the back of a knife or a heavy object, this will help release the natural flavours.
2. Pour the water into a large pot, add the lemongrass and ginger. Cover and bring to the boil, then reduce to a medium heat and simmer for 15 minutes.
3. Remove the lemongrass and ginger pieces.
4. Stir in the sugar until it has dissolved.
5. Allow to cool for an hour then transfer to the fridge to cool completely.
6. Serve over ice.

Chapter 4
Indianish

Indian BBQ Chicken with Peach Raspberry Salad

Ingredients:

- 2 tbsp sunflower oil
- 8 chicken thighs or pieces
- salt and freshly ground black pepper

Basting sauce:
- 4 tbsp apple cider vinegar
- 4 tbsp dark brown sugar
- 4 tbsp Dijon mustard
- 4 tbsp honey
- 1 tsp medium or hot curry powder
- 1 tsp ground allspice
- salt and freshly ground black pepper

Salad:
- 4 fresh peaches, sliced into wedges
- 1/2 cucumber, peeled into ribbons with a vegetable peeler
- 200g raspberries
- 50g flaked almonds, toasted
- 2 tbsp fresh coconut shavings

Dressing:
- 5 tbsp grapeseed oil
- 2 tbsp raspberry vinegar
- 1 tsp shop-bought mint jelly
- salt and freshly ground black pepper

Serves 8

Method:

1. Mix all the basting sauce ingredients together.
2. Lightly oil the chicken with sunflower oil and season well with salt and pepper. Grill on all sides on a hot BBQ until well sealed and crispy. Baste the chicken liberally, then move to a medium-hot part of the BBQ and continue to grill for 30–35 minutes, until cooked through.
3. Mix all the dressing ingredients together and season to taste with salt and pepper.
4. Gently mix all the salad ingredients together and drizzle with the dressing. Divide between the plates and serve with a piece of chicken.

Allspice, often confused with mixed spice, is a secret weapon Pantry Pal. A pinch of this spice will transform meatballs, burgers, stews and BBQ sauces. It has an interesting savoury, aromatic flavour that gives food an extra dimension without being distinguishable in the overall flavour. Dried spices keep well for 6 months if well sealed, then they start losing their pungency.

Yoghurt-marinated Spiced Lamb and Chickpea Salad

Ingredients:

- 2 cloves of garlic, crushed
- 80ml (1/3 cup) Greek yoghurt
- 2 tsp grated fresh ginger
- 1 tsp garam masala
- 1/2 tsp ground turmeric
- 4 thick lamb steaks or side loin lamb chops
- light olive oil
- salt and freshly ground black pepper

Chickpea salad:
- 2 x 400g tins of chickpeas, rinsed and drained
- 1 red onion, finely sliced
- 60ml (1/4 cup) extra virgin olive oil, plus extra for cooking
- 1/2 tsp cumin seeds
- 1/2 tsp fennel seeds
- 1/2 tsp black mustard seeds
- 2 tbsp white wine vinegar
- 1 tsp caster sugar
- salt and freshly ground black pepper
- 1/2 cucumber, peeled, seeded and cut into 1cm dice
- 100g cherry tomatoes, halved
- 100g baby salad leaves
- 15g (1/2 cup) small coriander leaves

Serves 4

Method:

1. Combine the garlic, yoghurt, ginger, garam masala and turmeric in a bowl. Rub this spice mixture over the lamb, cover and refrigerate for 2 hours.
2. To make the salad, toss the chickpeas with the sliced onion, olive oil, cumin seeds, fennel seeds, black mustard seeds, vinegar and sugar. Season with salt and pepper and set aside.
3. Scrape the marinade off the lamb and coat with light olive oil. Season well with salt and pepper, then cook for 4 minutes on each side on a hot BBQ. Rest the lamb for 5 minutes, loosely covered with foil.
4. Add the cucumber, tomatoes, baby salad leaves and coriander to the chickpea salad and toss to combine. Cut the lamb diagonally into thin slices, then layer with salad in bowls. Serve immediately.

Garam masala is a traditional blend of ground aromatic spices used alone or with other seasonings. Combinations vary, but typically garam masala will contain black and white pepper, cloves, cinnamon, cumin seeds and cardamom. Some versions also contain nutmeg. Make up your own garam masala by toasting whole spices and grinding them up or buy from an authentic source.

Coronation Chicken Salad

Ingredients:

- 4 chicken breasts
- 2 tbsp sunflower oil
- 1 tbsp mild curry powder
- salt and freshly ground black pepper
- 6 stalks of celery, very finely chopped
- 300g red seedless grapes, halved
- 100g cashew nuts
- 1 punnet micro salad, pea shoots or alfalfa sprouts
- 2 heads of baby Cos lettuces, leaves carefully separated

Dressing:
- 125ml mayonnaise
- 125ml sour cream
- 100ml mango chutney (chopped up if chunky)
- 2 tbsp medium curry powder

Serves 6

Method:

1. Rub the chicken with the oil, curry powder, salt and pepper. Grill on a medium-hot BBQ for 20–25 minutes, until cooked through.
2. Allow to rest for 10 minutes, then slice the chicken on the diagonal. Allow to cool completely before adding to your salad.
3. Mix all the dressing ingredients together very well.
4. Mix the cooled chicken, celery, grapes, cashews and half the micro salad with the dressing. Serve in the lettuce leaves and garnish with the rest of the micro salad.

Mango chutney is an essential Pantry Pal and is one of many types of chutneys and preserves in Indian cooking. It can used as a condiment with a curry, mixed in to form a sauce and is excellent as a marinade or baste, especially on BBQ chicken. Even your traditional Sunday roast chicken can benefit from a bit of a chutney baste!

Fake Away Tandoori Prawns and Salad

Ingredients:

- 20 tiger prawns, shelled, headed and veined
- 2 mangos, peeled and sliced
- 2 papayas, peeled, seeded and sliced
- 1 bunch of spring onions, finely sliced
- 1/2 cucumber, finely sliced
- juice of 2 limes
- salt and freshly ground black pepper
- pinch of chilli flakes

Marinade:
- 2 cloves of garlic, crushed
- 1 thumb-sized piece of fresh ginger, finely grated
- 80g butter, melted
- juice of 2 lemons
- 1 tsp garam masala
- 1 tsp red chilli powder
- 1 tsp ground cumin
- 1 tsp ground coriander
- 1/2 tsp turmeric
- 1/2 tsp tandoori masala

Serves 4

Method:

1. Soak 4 bamboo skewers in cold water for 1 hour.
2. Mix together all the ingredients for the marinade, reserving 2 tablespoons for basting. Stir in the prawns and marinate for 20 minutes.
3. Thread the prawns onto the bamboo skewers or place in a wire BBQ 'sandwich' rack, which makes them easier to turn.
4. Grill the prawns on a hot BBQ for 8–10 minutes, basting regularly with the reserved sauce, until the prawns are pink and firm – they don't take long.
5. Mix together the mangos, papayas, spring onions and cucumber. Season well with lime juice, salt and pepper and a sprinkling of chilli flakes. Serve with the hot prawns.

Tandoori masala is a traditional spice blend used to season meat, especially chicken, before it's roasted in a tandoor, a traditional clay oven that can reach very high temperatures. This gives a wonderful charred effect to the meat, a bit like a BBQ would. Tandoori spice has a distinctive red colour from chilli powder and cayenne pepper, and sometimes annatto or food colouring.

Spicy Lentil Veggie Burgers

Ingredients:

- 250ml (1 cup) red lentils (use your measuring jug to measure by volume)
- 500ml (2 cups) vegetable stock
- sunflower oil
- 2 medium carrots, grated
- 2 medium courgettes, skin on, grated
- 1 medium onion, grated
- 1 clove of garlic, crushed
- 1 tbsp medium curry powder
- 60g (1/2 cup) self-raising flour
- 250ml (1 cup) oat bran (use your measuring jug to measure by volume)
- salt and freshly ground black pepper

To serve:
- pita pockets
- tomato and onion sambal
- chutney
- fresh coriander

Serves 4

Method:

1. Add the lentils and stock to a pot. Bring to a boil, then reduce to a simmer for 25 minutes, until just cooked. Set aside to cool a little.
2. Heat a little oil in a pan over a medium heat. Gently sauté the carrots, courgettes, onion and garlic for 8 minutes, until softened. Add the curry powder and stir until fragrant. Set aside and allow to cool a little.
3. Combine the veggies, lentils, flour and oat bran and mix well. Season with salt and pepper.
4. Dust a little flour onto a chopping board and shape the mixture into 4–6 fat patties.
5. Heat a little sunflower oil in a pan over a medium-high heat and fry the burgers until they're golden on one side before flipping over and cooking until golden and crispy on the other side. Serve with pita pockets, tomato and onion sambal, chutney and fresh coriander.

Red lentils are a wonderful Pantry Pal, packed with nutrients and texture. Lentils, split peas and chickpeas are widely used in Indian cooking and they marry well with Indian spices. All lentils have a different texture when cooked: red lentils go quite mushy and creamy and are ideal to add to soups for protein and bulk. They keep well stored in an airtight container.

Indian Spiced Potato Cake

Ingredients:

- 4 large potatoes, peeled and quartered
- 40g butter, softened
- 1 tsp curry powder
- salt and freshly ground black pepper
- 4 spring onions, finely chopped
- 150g (1 cup) roasted cashews, roughly chopped
- 2 tsp lemon zest
- 2 tsp orange zest
- 4 egg whites, stiffly whipped

Makes 1 cake

Method:

1. Preheat the oven to 180°C. Grease and line a 23cm springform cake tin with greaseproof paper.
2. Boil the potatoes in a large pot of salted water until just cooked. Drain well in a colander and mash with the butter and curry powder until smooth. Season well with salt and pepper and set aside to cool.
3. Add the spring onions, cashews and lemon and orange zest to the cooled mash and mix well. Gently fold in the stiffly beaten egg whites.
4. Transfer the mixture to the cake tin and bake for 30–40 minutes, until golden. Serve warm.

Curry powder is in fact a British invention. In India, a vast array of spice blends are used, the closest to our Western curry powder being sambar powder. Curry powders available in supermarkets tend to be pretty standard and come in mild, medium and hot versions. Curry powder is great as a seasoning to add a little kick to a dish without overpowering it. Use in conjunction with other spices for your Indian cooking.

Mango Peppadew Salad

Ingredients:

- 8 peppadews, halved
- 1 large mango, peeled and diced
- 1 yellow pepper, seeded and finely diced
- 1 bunch of spring onions, finely chopped
- 1/2 cucumber, sliced into ribbons
- 1/2 pomegranate, seeds only
- 250g baby spinach, washed and dried
- 2 tbsp chopped fresh coriander

Dressing:
- 4 tbsp rapeseed oil
- 2 tbsp balsamic vinegar
- 1 tsp honey
- salt and freshly ground black pepper

Serves 6 as a side salad

Method:

1. Mix all the dressing ingredients together and check for seasoning. Set aside.
2. Mix together all the salad ingredients in a large bowl. Toss with the dressing just before serving.

Peppadews are a type of sweet, piquant pepper native to the Limpopo region of South Africa. They were first discovered in 1993 and are now readily available in jars in a sweet pickling liquid. Peppadews come in mild and hot varieties and are ideal added to a dish for a little heat without the need to use fresh chillies. A handy Pantry Pal to dolly up salads, chorizo bean stews, quesadillas or huevos rancheros or to serve with prawns or as a canapé.

Pistachio Pomegranate Rice Salad

Ingredients:

- 125ml (1/2 cup) basmati rice (use your measuring jug to measure by volume)
- 1 tsp caster sugar
- zest and juice of 1 lemon
- 75ml olive oil
- salt and freshly ground black pepper
- 1 ripe pomegranate, seeds only
- 1/2 red onion, finely sliced
- 50g pistachio nuts
- handful of fresh coriander, chopped

Serves 4

Method:

1. Rinse the rice in a colander, then cook in 750ml boiling salted water until just tender. Rinse in cold water and drain well. Spread out and allow to cool completely.
2. Dissolve the sugar in the lemon juice, then whisk in the oil. Pour over the rice and season well with salt and pepper.
3. Mix the pomegranate seeds, sliced red onion and pistachio nuts through the rice. Garnish with lemon zest and coriander.

Pistachio nuts are one of my favourite nuts. With their bright green colour and unique, naturally savoury taste, they can be used in both savoury and sweet dishes. While shelling them can be therapeutic, if you need large quantities for a recipe, buy them unshelled and freeze them to retain their freshness. Enjoy them in salads, in biscuit bases for desserts and with a cheese board.

Curried Quinoa and Roasted Butternut Squash

Ingredients:

- 2 red onions, peeled and sliced into wedges
- 1 butternut squash, peeled and diced
- 2 tbsp olive oil
- 1 tsp fennel seeds
- 1 tsp freshly grated nutmeg
- salt and freshly ground black pepper
- 350g (2 cups) quinoa
- 3 tsp medium curry powder
- 1 tsp garam masala
- 1 litre (4 cups) low-salt chicken or vegetable stock
- 1 x 400g tin of chickpeas, rinsed and drained
- 200g baby spinach leaves
- juice of 1 lemon

Serves 4

Method:

1. Coat the onions and butternut squash with the olive oil, fennel seeds and nutmeg and season with salt and pepper. Grill on a medium-hot BBQ for about 20 minutes, until charred and softened.
2. Place the quinoa, curry powder, garam masala and stock in a pot and bring to the boil. Add in the rinsed chickpeas and reduce to a simmer for 15 minutes, until the quinoa is light and fluffy and all the stock has been absorbed. Season with black pepper.
3. Stir in the spinach by the handful until it wilts down.
4. Plate up the quinoa with the roasted butternut squash and red onions piled on top. Squeeze over fresh lemon juice to taste.

Quinoa is the fruit of a plant native to Bolivia, but it looks and cooks like a grain. Gluten free and a perfect protein, quinoa is one of the healthiest Pantry Pals I stock. A great source of fibre, quinoa is very easy to cook and goes well with most cuisines. It has a lovely texture, a slight nutty taste and it absorbs flavours and sauces well. Use as a base for satisfying salads.

Easy Peasy Piccalilli

Ingredients:

- 400g cauliflower, chopped into small florets
- 400g courgettes, sliced into rings
- 400g carrots, sliced into rings
- 400g green beans, cut into short lengths
- 300g small shallots, peeled and halved
- 200g cherry tomatoes, left whole
- 100g free-flowing salt

Pickling spice:
- 60g cornflour
- 1 tbsp English mustard powder
- 1 tbsp ground turmeric
- 1 tbsp ground ginger
- 1 tbsp yellow mustard seeds
- 2 tsp crushed cumin seeds
- 2 tsp crushed coriander seeds
- 400g granulated sugar
- 1.2 litres apple cider vinegar
- 2 bay leaves

Make 2 x 500ml jars

Method:

1. Place a large colander over a bowl or in the sink. Layer up the veggies in the colander, salting very well between each layer. Place a plate on top and weigh it down with a couple of tins. Leave for at least 24 hours, then rinse the veggies very well and drain.
2. Remove the rubber seal from Kilner jars and wash the jars in hot soapy water. Rinse very well in clean water and place upside on the oven shelf. Bake for 10 minutes at 150°C to dry and sterilise the jars.
3. Mix the cornflour, English mustard, turmeric, ginger, mustard seeds, cumin and coriander with a little water until it forms a smooth paste.
4. Pour the sugar and vinegar into a saucepan and slowly bring to the boil, stirring to dissolve the sugar. Add the spice paste, whisking well, and boil for a few minutes, until the sauce thickens. Add in the bay leaves.
5. Remove from the heat and mix with the prepared vegetables. Bottle immediately in the clean, sterilised jars. Allow to mature for 6 weeks and use within 6 months. Store in a cool, dark place.

Turmeric, with its distinctive intense yellow colour, is an essential Indian Pantry Pal. Lending colour and warmth to dishes, turmeric has been proven to have fantastic antioxidant and anti-inflammatory properties. Buy turmeric from an Asian market or speciality brand for a truly pungent product.

Mango and Passionfruit Cheesecake

Ingredients:

- 200g coconut biscuits
- 80g butter, melted
- 3 fresh mangoes
- 5 fresh passionfruit
- juice of 2 limes
- 200g cream cheese
- 125g caster sugar
- 175ml Greek yoghurt
- 25ml gelatine
- edible flowers, to decorate

Serves 8

Method:

1. Grease and line a 20cm round springform baking tin.
2. Put the biscuits in a ziplock bag and crush with a rolling pin or blitz them in a food processor. Transfer the crumbs to a bowl and stir in the melted butter. Tip into the baking tin and press down. Allow the base to set in the fridge for 20 minutes.
3. Peel and chop 2 of the mangos, then place in a food processor and blitz until it becomes a smooth purée. Stir in the pulp from 3 of the passionfruit and the lime juice. Set aside.
4. Beat together the cream cheese and sugar, then add in the yoghurt and mango passionfruit purée.
5. Pour 60ml boiling water into a bowl. Sprinkle over the gelatine and leave to dissolve and cool for 15 minutes, then stir into the cheesecake mixture.
6. Carefully pour the cheesecake filling into the biscuit-lined tin. Leave to set in the fridge for 4 hours.
7. Release the cheesecake from the springform tin. Scoop out the pulp from the remaining 2 passionfruit and peel and slice the remaining mango. Decorate the cheesecake with the passionfruit pulp, sliced mango and edible flowers.

Passionfruit in South Africa is known granadilla. This small fruit is packed with sweet sour zingy pulp that you scrape out with a teaspoon. Delicious simply over ice cream or fruit salad, or in desserts like cheesecake and meringue. Fantastic in cocktails and coolers, this little fruit packs a punch. Look out for tinned passionfruit pulp and passionfruit juice.

Coconut and Mango Lassi

Ingredients:

- 1 1/2 cup coconut water
- 1 cup fresh or tinned mango
- 2 tbsp plain yoghurt
- 1 tbsp fresh lime juice
- 100ml coconut liqueur or Malibu rum
- edible flowers, to garnish

Serves 4

Method:

1. Blend together the coconut water, mango, yoghurt and lime until very smooth.
2. Chill for an hour.
3. Mix very well, pour into 4 glasses and top up with a shot of coconut liqueur. Garnish with edible flowers.

Chai Iced Tea

Ingredients:

- 4 orange pekoe tea bags or 4 tbsp of loose tea
- 1.5 litres of boiling water
- 1/2 cup sugar
- 1 cinnamon stick
- 1 thumb ginger, peeled and grated
- 2 cloves
- 2 cardamom pods, bruised
- 1/4 tsp fennel seeds
- 500ml water
- orange slices, to serve
- fresh mint, to serve

Serves 8

Method:

1. Pour the boiling water over the tea and leave to infuse for 5 minutes.
2. Remove the tea bags or strain if using loose tea. Stir in the sugar to dissolve.
3. In a pot, combine the cinnamon stick, ginger, cloves, cardamom and fennel. Bring to the boil then reduce to a simmer for 15 minutes. Strain and add to the tea.
4. Allow the tea to cool for an hour then place in the fridge until completely chilled.
5. Serve with orange slices and fresh mint.

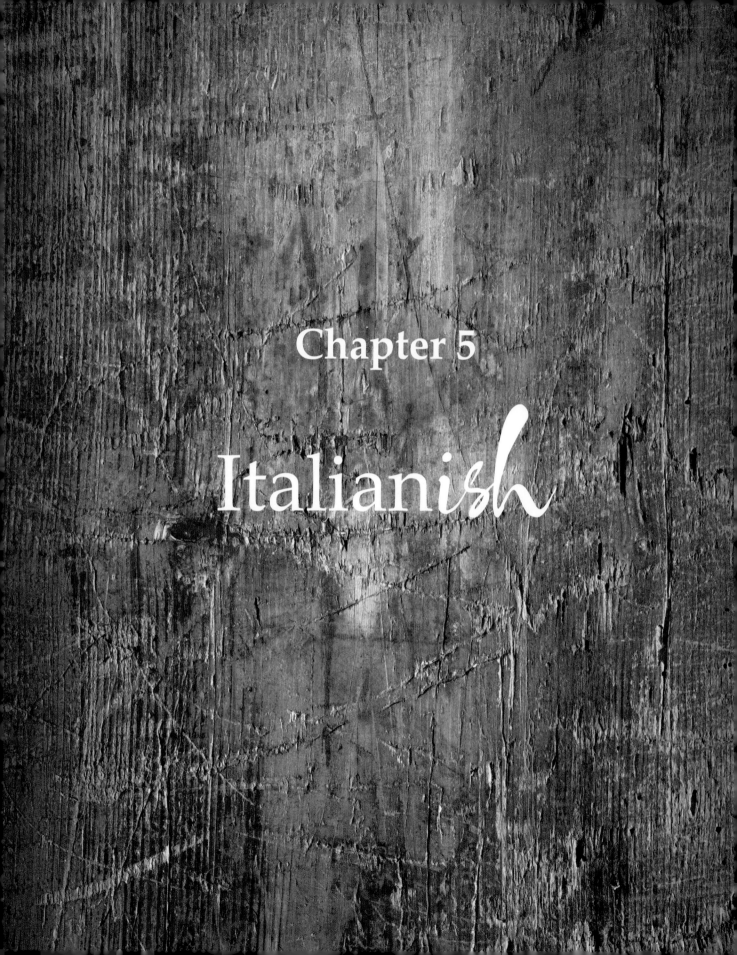

Chapter 5

Italian*ish*

Norman's Butterflied Leg of Lamb with Lively Salsa

Ingredients:

- 100g sundried tomatoes, chopped
- 6 cloves of garlic, crushed
- 1 small tin of anchovies, roughly chopped
- 2 tbsp finely chopped fresh rosemary
- 100ml olive oil
- juice and zest of 1 lemon
- 1.5kg leg of lamb, deboned

Salsa:
- 12 green olives, roughly chopped
- 6 tinned anchovy fillets, chopped
- 1 clove of garlic, crushed
- 6 tbsp chopped fresh flat leaf parsley
- 6 tbsp chopped fresh basil
- 6 tbsp chopped fresh mint
- 1 tbsp capers
- 10 tbsp extra virgin olive oil
- 6 tbsp red wine vinegar
- 1 tbsp lemon juice
- 1 tsp Dijon mustard
- salt and freshly ground black pepper

Serves 6–8

Method:

1. Blitz or mix the sundried tomatoes, garlic, anchovies, rosemary, olive oil and lemon juice together and rub it into the lamb. Cover and refrigerate overnight to marinate.
2. Mix all the salsa ingredients together, cover and refrigerate.
3. Place the marinated lamb on a hot grill, fat facing down. Cover with foil and seal well for 5–6 minutes. Turn over, cover with foil and seal the other side for 5–6 minutes.
4. Cook the lamb for a further 15–20 minutes on each side. Allow to rest, covered in foil, for 10 minutes before serving.
5. Serve thick slices of the lamb with generous dollops of the lively salsa.

Anchovies can be bought in tins or glass bottles, preserved in salt and oil. They are an indispensable Pantry Pal in Italian cooking. They melt into dishes, imparting a rich, salty, savoury flavour, you wont have any bones or fishiness. Don't be put off, as they aren't fishy and really work. Be brave – try them!

Limoncello Chicken and Citrus Salad

Ingredients:

- 4 large skinless, boneless chicken breasts
- light olive oil
- juice of 1 lemon
- salt and freshly ground black pepper
- 2 oranges
- 2 lemons

Basting sauce:
- 4 tbsp marmalade
- 4 tbsp limoncello liqueur
- 4 tbsp olive oil
- 1 tbsp wholegrain mustard
- salt and freshly ground black pepper

Salad:
- 150g rocket leaves
- 30g pine nuts
- 30g dried cranberries
- 2 tbsp freshly chopped flat leaf parsley

Salad dressing:
- juice of 1 lemon
- 4 tbsp olive oil
- 1 tsp Dijon mustard
- 1 tsp honey
- salt and freshly ground black pepper

Serves 4 as a main dish

Method:

1. Mix all the salad dressing ingredients together and season to taste. I like my dressing quite tart, so I use a lot of lemon. You might prefer less lemon or a touch more honey.
2. Score 3 diagonal lines across the fattest part of each chicken breast. This will allow the chicken to cook slightly faster. Brush the chicken with the light olive oil and season with a squeeze of lemon juice, salt and pepper.
3. Mix together the marmalade, limoncello, olive oil and mustard, then season well with salt and pepper.
4. Cut the oranges and lemons into 2cm-thick slices. Try to flick out as many of the pips as you can.
5. Place the chicken on a hot grill and seal for 3–4 minutes on each side, until well browned and golden. Only turn the chicken once it's sealed on the first side, otherwise it will stick and shred. Baste with the sauce, then move to a medium-hot part of the grill and cook for a further 10–12 minutes, basting all the time. The chicken should feel firm when squeezed and no pink should be visible when it's cut open. Remove the chicken from the grill when it's done and allow to rest for 5 minutes, then slice into thick diagonal slices.
6. Lightly oil the orange and lemon slices and place them on the grill. Turn them over once the fruit is charred and grill the other side. Remove from the BBQ and set aside.
7. Gently mix the rocket leaves, pine nuts, dried cranberries and parsley in a bowl. Divide between 4 plates, then arrange the chicken slices and charred orange and lemon slices on top. Drizzle over the dressing.

Limoncello is a traditional lemon liqueur made in southern Italy using the highly prized local lemons. The fragrant lemon zest is steeped in grain alcohol until the essential oils are released. This lemon-infused liquid is then mixed with a sugar syrup to perfect the favour. Why not try making your own as a fun foodie project?

Panko Parmesan Scallops with Grilled Asparagus

Ingredients:

- 100g panko breadcrumbs
- 50g Parmesan cheese, grated
- zest of 1 lemon
- 4–5 tbsp olive oil
- salt and freshly ground black pepper
- 20 large scallops

Grilled asparagus:
- 2 bunches of asparagus
- olive oil
- salt and freshly ground black pepper
- extra virgin olive oil
- Parmesan shavings
- lemon wedges

Serves 4 as a main dish

Method:

1. Mix together the panko breadcrumbs, Parmesan cheese, lemon zest and olive oil. Season well with salt and pepper.
2. Press the scallops firmly into the breadcrumb mixture and coat well. Place on a wire rack and chill in the fridge for at least 20 minutes to help set the breadcrumbs.
3. On a hot BBQ grill or hotplate, cook the scallops on one side for 2–3 minutes, until golden. Turn and brown the other side. Do not overcook, as scallops cook very quickly.
4. Lightly coat the asparagus with olive oil and season with salt and pepper. Grill until nicely charred.
5. Dress the asparagus with a drizzle of extra virgin olive oil, some Parmesan shavings and lemon wedges on the side. Serve the asparagus hot with the golden scallops.

Parmesan cheese is an indispensable Italian ingredient. You can freeze well-wrapped wedges of Parmesan so that you always have it to hand. Panko breadcrumbs are Japanese breadcrumbs made with rice flakes, which give the crispiest, crunchiest breadcrumb coating. Panko are very dry and crispy and should stay fresh in the pantry, but of in doubt, freeze the bag for future use.

BBQ Peaches and Parma Ham with Strawberry Chilli Dressing

Ingredients:

- 20 thinly sliced pieces of Parma ham, torn into large strips
- 4 peaches, cut into large wedges
- olive oil
- freshly ground black pepper
- 4 balls of fresh buffalo mozzarella
- 150g baby salad leaves, such as baby spinach, beetroot and lamb's lettuce

Dressing:
- 150g fresh strawberries, hulled and sliced
- 1 tbsp caster sugar
- 1 tbsp balsamic vinegar
- 1 small red chilli, seeded and diced
- salt and freshly ground black pepper
- 2 tbsp finely chopped basil leaves

Serves 4

Method:

1. To make the dressing, mix all the dressing ingredients together except the fresh basil. Leave at room temperature to infuse, as the flavours will be so much better.
2. Wrap the Parma ham around the peach wedges. Lightly coat with olive oil and season with black pepper.
3. On a medium-hot BBQ, grill the peaches until the Parma ham is crispy and the edges of the peaches are caramelised.
4. Add the basil to the dressing just before serving.
5. Serve the grilled peaches with torn buffalo mozzarella, baby salad leaves and the strawberry and chilli dressing.

Parma ham is now widely available, but few people realise that this traditionally cured ham is fiercely protected by the Parma Ham Consortium, which legislates and regulates the production and quality of this prized cured meat. Only 161 firms in Italy produce this ham and each bears the emblem of the Ducal Crown to prove authenticity and quality. Crisp up Parma ham in a dry non stick pan as a low fat alternative to crispy bacon for brekkie.

Lee-Ann's Salami and Strawberry Crostini

Ingredients:

- 1 loaf of ciabatta bread, cut into 1.5cm slices
- 200g salami (about 20–24 slices)
- 200g mozzarella cheese (the firm variety you grate for pizza), sliced
- 12–14 fresh strawberries, hulled and halved
- balsamic vinegar reduction (see Ish Factor below)
- freshly ground black pepper

Serves 8 as a canapé

Method:

1. Top the ciabatta slices with a slice of salami and then a slice of cheese. Grill on a BBQ or under an oven grill until the bread is lightly toasted and the cheese has melted.
2. Place half a strawberry on top of each crostini and drizzle over some balsamic vinegar reduction. Season with freshly ground black pepper.
3. Serve immediately while still warm.

Balsamic vinegar reduction or glaze is simply balsamic vinegar that has been reduced down until the moisture has evaporated and it becomes thick and syrupy. Simply simmer 500ml of balsamic vinegar vigorously until it has reduced by at least two-thirds. You can also add in black peppercorns and a bay leaf while simmering. It's delicious as a glaze over meats or drizzled over salads and fresh strawberries. Keep in a plastic squeezy bottle for easy application as a garnish.

Slow Roasted Tomato Pesto

Ingredients:

- 5 large tomatoes
- salt and freshly ground black pepper
- 3 sprigs of fresh thyme
- 50g Parmesan cheese, grated
- 50g pine nuts, lightly toasted
- 2 cloves of garlic
- 75ml olive oil
- squeeze of lemon juice
- cayenne pepper (optional)

Makes 1 bowl

Method:

1. Preheat the oven to 120°C. Grease a large baking tray.
2. Thinly slice the tomatoes and evenly arrange them on the baking tray. Season well with salt and pepper and scatter over the plucked fresh thyme leaves.
3. Bake for 1 1/2 hours, stirring once. The tomato slices will be dehydrated and semi-dry. Alternatively, if you have a BBQ with a lid, place the tray of tomatoes on the BBQ straight after cooking something else, close the lid and leave them overnight.
4. To make the pesto, blend the roasted tomatoes with all of the remaining ingredients in a food processor. Adjust the seasoning to taste with the lemon juice, salt, pepper and cayenne.
5. Store in an airtight container in the fridge for 4–5 days.

This recipe is the homemade version of making your own sundried tomato pesto – one of the most useful ingredients in my pantry. Spread onto sandwiches, quesadillas or pizza bases or mix with olive oil as a base for grilled fish or chicken. The uses are endless!

Pizza Polenta Bread

Ingredients:

- 500ml polenta or maize meal (use your measuring jug to measure by volume)
- 250ml cake flour or plain flour
- 2 tsp baking powder
- 2 tsp dried oregano
- 1 tsp bicarbonate of soda (bread soda)
- 3 eggs
- 100g butter, melted
- 250ml sour cream

Pizza toppings:
- 2 red peppers,
- 200g pepperoni or salami, roughly chopped
- 100g (1 cup) grated mozzarella
- 100g (1 cup) grated mature cheddar
- 100g feta cheese, crumbled
- 2 red onions, very finely sliced into rings

Makes 2 loaves

Method:

1. Grill halved red peppers over an open flame or under the oven grill until well charred. Place in a glass bowl covered in cling film and allow to sweat for 10 minutes. Peel off the charred skin and discard with the seeds.
2. Preheat the oven to 180°C. Grease and line a 20cm round cake tin.
3. Sift all the dry ingredients into a large mixing bowl.
4. In a separate bowl, thoroughly mix the eggs, melted butter and sour cream and add to the dry ingredients. Before stirring, add half the peppers, half the pepperoni or salami, half the mozzarella, half the cheddar and half the feta cheese. Mix until completely combined, but don't over mix. It will look lumpy and that's fine.
5. Pour the batter into the tin. Sprinkle over the remaining peppers, pepperoni or salami, mozzarella, cheddar and feta cheese. Arrange the red onion rings on top and press down lightly.
6. Bake for 40–50 minutes, until an inserted skewer comes out clean.
7. Allow to cool in the tin for 5–10 minutes before turning out onto a wire rack to cool.

Polenta is a type of finely milled maize meal that can be used in bread and cakes. You can also make it into a smooth paste that can be served with milk and sugar as a porridge or as a savoury side dish with herbs and grated Parmesan cheese. Polenta is widely used in Italian baking, especially for lemon and chocolate cakes.

Berry, Blue Cheese and Radicchio Salad

Ingredients:

- 40g flaked almonds
- 30g pine nuts
- 2 heads of radicchio
- 200g strawberries, hulled and halved
- 100g blueberries
- 50g Cape gooseberries, halved
- 1 stalk of celery, finely sliced
- 100g blue cheese, crumbled
- zest of 1/2 orange

Dressing:
- 100ml extra virgin olive oil
- 30ml white balsamic vinegar
- juice of 1/2 orange
- 1 tsp honey
- 1 tsp Dijon mustard
- salt and freshly ground black pepper

Serves 8 as a side dish

Method:

1. Lightly toast the flaked almond and pine nuts in a dry pan. Be careful not to burn them – aim for a pale golden colour. Set aside to cool.
2. Divide the radicchio into separate leaves, discarding any discoloured bits. Gently combine with the strawberries, blueberries, gooseberries and celery. Crumble over the blue cheese, then zest the orange directly over the salad.
3. Whisk all the dressing ingredients together until emulsified. Taste the dressing and adjust the flavours to your liking.
4. Just before serving, drizzle the dressing over the salad and scatter over the toasted almonds and pine nuts.

Pine nuts are widely used in Italian cooking, even as a crunchy topping for lemon polenta cakes or tarts. They are very expensive, and unfortunately are often borderline stale when you buy them. Freeze airtight bags of pine nuts to retain the freshness and lightly toast them on a clean, dry pan until golden to revive the nutty flavour. You can do the same with the flaked almonds or any other nut or seed.

Grilled Summer Veg Panzanella Salad

Ingredients:

- olive oil
- 4 vine-ripened tomatoes, halved
- 4 sprigs of fresh thyme or
  1 tsp dried thyme
- salt and freshly ground
  black pepper
- 2 red peppers, deseeded
  and quartered
- 2 yellow peppers, deseeded
  and quartered
- 2 courgettes, sliced into long
  strips about 1cm thick
- 2 red onions, peeled and sliced
  into thick rings
- 1 aubergine, sliced into
  1.5cm slices
- 1 loaf of ciabatta, torn into
  chunky pieces
- 1 whole garlic bulb
- 125ml (1/2 cup) black olives
- 50ml (1/4 cup) capers
- large bunch of basil leaves

Dressing:
- 4 tbsp extra virgin olive oil
- 2 tbsp balsamic vinegar
- salt and freshly ground
  black pepper

Serves 8 as a side dish

Method:

1. Drizzle a little olive oil on the cut side of the tomatoes. Scatter over the fresh or dried thyme and season with salt and pepper.
2. In a large bowl, gently toss together the pepper quarters, courgette strips and onion rings with a little olive oil. Season well with salt and pepper.
3. Using a pastry brush, lightly brush both sides of the aubergine slices with olive oil, then season with salt and pepper.
4. Arrange the bread, tomatoes, peppers, courgettes, onions, aubergine and the whole garlic bulb on a medium-hot grill. Toast the bread until golden and crunchy, then remove it from the BBQ.
5. Gently cook the tomatoes until they start to wrinkle underneath. Remove them from the grill and chop into quarters, capturing all the juice in a bowl.
6. Turn the peppers, courgettes, onions and aubergine when they have prominent grill marks underneath. Remove the garlic bulb once it feels soft when squeezed.
7. In a large bowl, mix the toasted bread with the grilled tomatoes and their juices, peppers, courgettes, onions, aubergine, olives and capers.
8. To make the dressing, mix the olive oil and balsamic vinegar together and season with salt and pepper. Squeeze two of the soft garlic cloves into the dressing and mix well. Separate the rest of the cloves and add them to the salad.
9. Pour the dressing over the salad and mix well. Scatter over the basil leaves just before serving.

Capers are the unripened flower buds of a prickly bush native to the Mediterranean. The larger caper berries, often left on the stalk, are the fruit. Once harvested, they're pickled in a briney liquid. Capers lend a wonderful tart and salty flavour to dressings, sauces and salads. Fry in a little oil for a crispy texture. A great Pantry Pal I always have on hand.

Fragrant Fennel Pickle

Ingredients:

- 3 x 500ml glass Kilner jars
- 10 fennel bulbs
- 3 small shallots, peeled and very finely sliced
- 1 large orange
- 6 whole star anise pods
- 5 tbsp coarse sea salt
- 2 tbsp sugar
- 500ml apple cider vinegar
- 250ml water

Makes 3 x 500ml jars

Method:

1. Remove the rubber seal from the glass jars and wash the jars in hot soapy water. Rinse very well in clean water and place upside on the oven shelf. Bake for 10 minutes at 150°C to dry and sterilise the jars.
2. Wash the fennel and cut away any bruises or brown spots. Discard the stalks and cut out the hard core at the base. You can keep the leaves for salads. Use a very sharp knife or a mandoline and slice the fennel into very thin rings. Mix the shallot slices with the fennel. Divide the fennel and shallots equally between the 3 glass jars.
3. Cut 6 wide strips of orange peel from the orange and trim away any white pith. Slide 2 pieces of orange peel down the side of each fennel-filled jar. Push 2 star anise pods into each jar.
4. Squeeze the juice from the orange into a pot. Add the salt, sugar, vinegar and water. Bring to the boil, stirring constantly until the sugar dissolves. Pour the hot pickling liquid over the fennel and shallots, ensuring they're completely covered. Push the fennel down if necessary.
5. Replace the rubber seal on the jars and close immediately. Allow to cool, then refrigerate. This will stay fresh for 3 days in the fridge. It's fantastic served with pork and white fish dishes or as a pickle with pâté.

Fennel always reminds me of Italy, where they even specify using male or female fennel in recipes. Male fennel has no 'hips' and is straight up and down, whereas female fennel has a rounded shape, hence 'hips'. You can cook fennel, but I love it raw. Thinly slice the bulb with a mandolin and use the fine leaves in salads. The tough stalks are good in a fish or chicken broth, but too tough to eat.

Francesca's Tiramisu Ice Cream

Ingredients:

- 2 tbsp instant espresso powder
- 2 tbsp boiling milk
- 2 tbsp coffee liqueur
- 2 tbsp Marsala liqueur
- 600ml double cream
- 1 x 397g tin condensed milk

Chocolate orange sauce:
- 200g dark chocolate (75% cocoa content)
- zest of 1/2 orange

Makes 1 dish

Method:

1. Dissolve the instant espresso powder in the boiling milk and mix well. Allow to cool completely.
2. Whisk the coffee, coffee liqueur and Marsala with the cream until soft peaks form. Add in the condensed milk and continue whisking until well combined. Pour into a 1-litre dish with a tight-fitting lid and freeze overnight.
3. To make the chocolate orange sauce, place a glass bowl over a pot of simmering water. Do not allow the water to touch the bowl. Break the chocolate into the bowl and zest the orange peel into the chocolate. Heat and stir until the chocolate is melted, smooth and shiny.
4. Serve the tiramisu ice cream with chocolate sauce and extra orange zest.

Marsala is a fortified wine produced in the city of Marsala in Sicily. It's my secret ingredient in my traditional tiramisu recipe, but it's equally delicious served chilled with a cheese board of pungent cheeses. Marsala is fantastic to deglaze a pan when making a sauce or gravy, especially for pork or chicken dishes. This Pantry Pal will certainly earn its keep.

Raspberry Aperol Prosecco

Ingredients:

- 1 bottle Aperol
- 1 bottel prosecco
- 1 bottle sparkling water
- 500g raspberries, frozen

Serves 10

Method:

1. Place a few raspberries at the bottom of each champagne glass.
2. Pour in 50ml of Aperol and lightly muddle.
3. Add 75ml of prosecco and top up with sparkling water.

Peach Earl Grey Iced Tea

Ingredients:

- 4 Earl Grey teabags or 4 tbsp loose tea
- 1 litre boiling water
- 1/2 cup honey
- 8 peaches, pitted and sliced
- Ice cubes, to serve

Serves 8

Method:

1. Pour the boling water over the tea and allow to infuse for 5 minutes.
2. Remove the teabags or strain if using loose tea. Stir in the honey to dissolve.
3. Add all the peach slices to the tea and allow to cool for an hour. Transfer to the fridge until completely chilled.
4. Serve well chilled with ice.

Chapter 6

Mozambique*ish*

Karen's Portuguese Steak with Spicy Wedges

Ingredients:

- 4 x 250g rib-eye or sirloin steaks
- 2 tbls sunflower oil
- 1 tbsp All Purpose Peri Peri sauce (page 153)
- coarse salt and freshly ground pepper
- rocket and coriander, to garnish
- fresh red chilli, to garnish

Sauce:
- 75g butter, melted and clarified
- 4 garlic cloves, crushed
- 75ml brandy
- 100ml red wine
- 100ml beef stock
- 2 tbsp crème fraiche

Spicy potato wedges:
- 8 rooster potatoes, scrubbed clean and cut into wedges
- 4 tbsp light olive oil
- 3 tbsp Cajun spice
- salt and freshly ground black pepper

Peri peri mayonnaise:
- 1 tbsp All Purpose Peri Peri sauce (page 153)
- 4 tbsp mayonnaise
- juice of 1/2 lemon

Serves 4

Method:

1. Coat the potato wedges with sunflower oil and season well with Cajun spice, salt and pepper. Spread out on a baking tray and bake in the oven at 220°C for 20 to 25 minutes until crispy and cooked through the middle.
2. Mix the peri peri mayonnaise and taste for seasoning. Add more peri peri if you like it hot.
3. Mix the sunflower oil and peri peri sauce and coat the four steaks. Season well with salt pepper. BBQ on a hot grill for three to four minutes a side for a rare to medium rare steak. Move to a medium hot part of the grill and cook further for a medium to well done steak.
4. In a cast iron skillet on the grill, add the clarified butter and garlic. Pour in the brandy and flambé. Add the red wine and beef stock and simmer until it reduced by half. Stir in the crème fraiche and season with salt and pepper. Dip each steak into the pan to coat well with the sauce before serving.
5. Plate up the steak with spicy potato wedges, peri peri mayonnaise and garnish with rocket and coriander and finely sliced red chilli.

Cajun spice is a mildly spicy seasoning that can be used on meat, seafood and veggies, it really is all purpose. Make your own by mixing: 2 tsp salt, 2 tsp garlic powder, 1 1/2 tsp paprika, 1 tsp ground black pepper, 1 1/2 tsp dried oregano, 1 1/2 tsp dried thyme, 1/2 tsp chilli flakes. Shake well and store in an airtight container for up to 6 months.

Strawberry Chilli Flattie Chicken

Ingredients:

- 1 x 1.9kg organic or free-range chicken
- 2 tbsp sunflower oil
- salt and freshly ground black pepper

Strawberry chilli baste:
- 100g butter
- juice of 1 lime
- 4 tbsp strawberry jam (seedless if possible)
- 2 tbsp balsamic vinegar glaze (see the recipe on page 117)
- 2 tbsp tomato paste
- 1 tbsp Worcestershire sauce
- 1 tsp hot paprika
- 1 tsp chilli flakes
- salt and freshly ground black pepper

Salad:
- 3 avocados, sliced and coated in lime juice to prevent discolouration
- 1 papaya, peeled and sliced
- 1 red onion, very finely sliced and marinated in the juice of 1 lime
- 250g (2 cups) strawberries, sliced
- 200g baby salad leaves
- 2 tbsp chopped fresh coriander

Dressing:
- 3 tbsp extra virgin olive oil
- 1 tbsp sherry vinegar
- 1 tsp honey
- pinch of chilli flakes
- salt and freshly ground black pepper

Serves 6

Method:

1. Melt together all the baste ingredients in a pot and season with salt and pepper. Divide in half.
2. With a pair of kitchen scissors, cut right through the undercarriage of the chicken carcass and open it out, into what is commonly called a spatchcock chicken. Oil the chicken with sunflower oil and season it with salt and pepper.
3. Place the chicken skin side down onto a medium-hot grill and brown for 8–10 minutes, until the skin is crispy. Just before you turn it over, baste the fleshy side very well with the strawberry chilli basting sauce.
4. Turn the chicken over. Baste with the sauce. Cover with foil and cook for 15 minutes.
5. Turn the chicken over and baste generously with the sauce. Cover with foil and grill for a further 15 minutes. Discard the rest of this half of the sauce.
6. With a sharp knife, slice into the thickest part of the chicken and check to see if you can see any pink. If you can see pink or the juices don't run clear, spritz and baste again with fresh sauce and cook for a further 10–15 minutes.
7. When the chicken is ready, loosely cover it with foil and allow it to rest before carving.
8. Whisk all the dressing ingredients together and season to taste.
9. Gently mix all the salad ingredients together and toss with the dressing. Serve with the BBQ chicken.

The Portuguese actually introduced paprika to Europe from their travels to the New World. Now it's one of the most beloved spices, with varieties ranging from sweet and mild to hot and fiery. For smoked paprika, the peppers are smoked over oak embers to give a distinctive smoky aroma and flavour. Smoked paprika is used across many cuisines and dishes, so it's definitely a good Pantry Pal.

Citrus Sumac Peri Peri Prawns

Ingredients:

- 20 large prawns, shell on but deveined
- juice of 1/2 lemon
- 1 tsp sumac
- 1 quantity All Purpose Mozambican Peri Peri Sauce (see page 153)
- 2 oranges, cut into wedges
- 2 lemons, cut into wedges
- sunflower oil

Serves 4

Method:

1. Wash and devein the prawns. Add the lemon juice and sumac to the All Purpose Mozambican Peri Peri Sauce. Coat the prawns in half the sauce and marinate in the fridge for 20 minutes.
2. Place the prawns straight on a medium-hot grill, or secure in a hinged wire BBQ rack or place in a cast iron skillet on top of the grill. Cook for 5–6 minutes on each side, until the prawns are a vivid coral colour, firm to the touch and have curled up.
3. Lightly oil the orange and lemon wedges. Place on the BBQ and grill until charred.
4. Serve the prawns hot with the other half of the Peri Peri Sauce and the charred orange and lemon wedges to squeeze over.

Sumac is the whole or ground dried berry of a Mediterranean bush. It's reddish-pink in colour and becomes more pink as it cooks, so don't be alarmed! Sumac is an astringent spice, so it enhances the flavour of other ingredients and on its own has a lemony taste. It goes particularly well with seafood, chicken, lamb, lentil, chickpea and aubergine dishes.

Chilli Garlic Baked Brie Bread

Ingredients:

- 1 small round sourdough loaf or 4 rolls
- 30g butter, softened
- salt and freshly ground black pepper
- 4 cloves of garlic, crushed
- 1 tbsp fresh oregano leaves
- 1 tsp chilli flakes
- 1/2 tsp English mustard powder
- 1 small wheel of Brie or Camembert cheese

Serves 8 as a starter

Method:

1. Measure the size of the bread in relation to the size of the cheese, then cut a circle in the top of the bread that's roughly the same size as the cheese. Hollow out a cavity for the cheese and scoop out the bread. (Use this bread to make croutons for salads and soups.)
2. Spread the butter inside the cavity and season well with salt and pepper. Sprinkle in half the garlic, oregano, chilli flakes and mustard powder.
3. Place the cheese in the cavity and sprinkle over the rest of the garlic, oregano, chilli flakes and mustard powder.
4. Wrap in foil and bake on a medium-hot BBQ until the cheese is melty.

English mustard powder is a seasoning and cooking condiment made from ground mustard seeds, turmeric and flour. It has a strong, sharp taste that is pungent rather than hot. You can also buy it ready prepared as a paste in a jar. I use English mustard to flavour salad dressings, marinades, basting sauces and any time a little oomph is required. It's a multipurpose Pantry Pal.

Cheesy Tuna Baked Potatoes

Ingredients:

- 8 large potatoes, scrubbed clean
- 3 tbsp olive oil
- salt and freshly ground black pepper

Tuna filling:
- 2 x 130g tins of tuna, drained
- 1 red onion, very finely chopped
- 1 green pepper, diced
- 1 red chilli, finely chopped
- 2 tbsp mayonnaise
- 1 tbsp chutney or relish
- 1 tbsp tomato ketchup

To garnish:
- 100g mature Cheddar cheese, grated
- 2 tbsp chopped fresh flat-leaf parsley
- 1 tsp paprika

Serves 8

Method:

1. Bring a large pot of salted water to the boil. Add in the potatoes and boil for 10 minutes. Drain, then wipe them dry with a clean tea towel.
2. Pierce each potato all over with a knife or fork. Rub with olive oil and season with salt and pepper. Wrap each potato in foil and nestle in the BBQ coals or place on top of a gas BBQ. Cook for roughly 40 minutes, turning twice, until the potato is soft when pierced with a blunt dinner knife.
3. Meanwhile, mix together all the tuna filling ingredients and set aside.
4. Unwrap each potato and score a cross into the top, cutting two-thirds of the way into it so that it opens up. Drizzle with a little olive oil and season with salt and pepper.
5. Pile the tuna filling on top of each potato. Top with grated cheese, fresh parsley and a sprinkling of paprika.

Tinned tuna is far from an exotic ingredient, but it's what you do with it that counts. Tuna packed in water is a figure-friendly, low-fat ingredient that's ideal for tuna melts, pasta bakes, wraps and quesadilla fillings. For a more gourmet treat, look for tuna packed in olive oil. It's more expensive, but worth it for special recipes.

Citrusy Fresh Carrot Salad

Ingredients:

- 30g sunflower seeds
- 30g flaked almonds
- 4 medium carrots
- 2 oranges
- 2 ruby grapefruits
- 2 ripe avocados
- juice of 1/2 lemon
- salt and freshly ground black pepper
- 30g roasted cashew nuts
- micro leaves or fresh coriander, to garnish

Dressing:
- 1 small red chilli, sliced
- juice of 1/2 lemon
- 2 tbsp avocado oil
- salt and freshly ground black pepper

Serves 8 as a side dish

Method:

1. Lightly toast the sunflower seeds and almond flakes in a clean, dry pan. Set aside to cool.
2. Peel and grate the carrots using a food processor or a box grater – choose the coarse grater attachment.
3. Peel the oranges and grapefruit and remove all the white pith. Either slice them up and flick out the pips, or segment the fruit by carefully cutting out each segment and discarding the rest.
4. Halve the avocadoes, pop out the stone and gently peel off the skin and discard it. Slice them up and coat generously with the lemon juice to prevent discolouration. Season with salt and pepper.
5. Mix the dressing and season to taste.
6. With clean hands, gently mix all the salad ingredients with the dressing and plate up. Garnish with extra herbs and toasted nuts and seeds.

Avocado oil is a lovely alternative to use in dressings when you don't want the unique, pungent taste of olive oil, the nutty taste of a rapeseed oil or a neutral oil like sunflower oil. The refined avocado oils are ideal for cooking and barbequing, as they can reach very high temperatures before burning (known as the smoke point). Buy dark glass bottles to preserve the oil's freshness and store in a cool, dark place.

Retro Rainbow Rice Salad

Ingredients:

- 250ml (1 cup) brown short grain brown rice (use your measuring jug to measure by volume)
- 3 tomatoes, finely diced
- 3 spring onions, finely chopped
- 2 stalks of celery, finely chopped
- 1 red pepper, finely chopped
- 1 green pepper, finely chopped
- 1 x 200g tin of sweetcorn
- 2 tbsp finely chopped fresh coriander, plus extra to garnish
- 2 tbsp chopped fresh chives
- 2 tbsp crème fraîche
- 2 tbsp olive oil
- 2 tbsp lemon juice
- 1 tbsp mayonnaise
- salt and freshly ground black pepper

Serves 4

Method:

1. Combine the rice and 625ml (2 1/2 cups) water in a pot. Bring to the boil, then reduce to a simmer with the lid askew until just tender – this will take 20–25 minutes. If you're using easy-cook rice, follow the cooking instructions on the bag.
2. Spread the cooked rice onto a clean tray and fan it to cool it down. Chill in the fridge for 1–2 hours. The rice must be completely cold, otherwise you'll breed bacteria.
3. Mix all the remaining ingredients with the cooled rice. Season with salt and pepper and garnish with extra coriander.

Brown rice is the unpolished grain whereby the seeds of the rice plant are milled to remove only the outer husks of the grain, and retaining the valuable bran. A powerhouse of valuable nutrients: soluble and insoluble fibre, vitamin E and B vitamins. Brown rice takes longer to cook than white, but the chewy texture and nutty taste is far more interesting and worth the wait.

Herby Summer Sweetcorn Salad

Ingredients:

- 2 cups sweetcorn (tinned, frozen, fresh from the cob)
- 1 tin kidney beans, rinsed and drained
- 1 red pepper, diced into small cubes
- 1 green pepper, diced into small cubes
- 1 courgette, skin on, diced into small cubes, like pepper
- 250g small plum tomatoes, halved
- 6 spring onions, sliced
- 1 cup of fresh mixed herbs: basil, coriander, oregano, thyme

Dressing:
- 1 clove garlic, crushed
- Juice of 2 limes
- 3 tbls olive oil
- Salt and pepper

Serves 8 as a side dish

Method:

1. For the dressing: mix together the ingredients and season to taste. I like lots of lime, so tend to use a little less olive oil. The dressing needs a good pinch of salt and pepper for all the veggies.
2. For the salad: dice the peppers and courgettes into a small blocks, mix with the sweetcorn, kidney beans and plum tomatoes, pour over the dressing.
3. Just before serving, sprinkle over the fresh herbs and spring onions.

Fresh herbs are an essential part of creating fresh, vibrant dishes. They can be expensive to buy, so do try growing a few pots, even if it's on a windowsill. When purchased, keep herbs fresh by lining a container with a clean, damp J cloth, layering your herbs gently then placing another damp cloth on top. Seal with a lid and keep in the fridge.

Portuguese Green Bean and Artichoke Salad

Ingredients:

- 500g green beans
- small jar of marinated artichoke hearts in oil
- 10 peppadews, sliced
- 1 x 400g tin cannellini beans, rinsed and drained
- 200g feta cheese, broken into small chunks
- 20g black olives
- fresh flat-leaf parsley, to garnish

Salad dressing:
- 100ml extra virgin olive oil
- 100ml red wine vinegar
- 1 clove of garlic, crushed
- 1 tbsp wholegrain mustard
- 1 tsp dried oregano
- salt and freshly ground black pepper

Herby croutons:
- 4 slices of leftover bread or rolls
- reserved oil from the jarred artichokes
- salt and freshly ground black pepper

Serves 8 as a side dish

Method:

1. Steam or blanch the green beans for 3 minutes. Plunge in ice water to refresh.
2. Lift the artichokes out of the oil in the jar and reserve the oil for the croutons.
3. To make the croutons, break the leftover bread into large pieces. Drizzle over some of the reserved oil from the artichokes and season well. Toast on a medium to hot BBQ until crispy or on a baking tray in the oven at 180°C until golden.
4. Mix together all the dressing ingredients. Taste and adjust the seasoning.
5. Toss together the green beans, artichokes, peppadews, cannellini beans, feta cheese and olives and drizzle with the dressing. Optional: place the artichoke hearts on a medium-hot BBQ and grill briefly, until charred.
6. Add the herby croutons just before serving so that they don't go soggy. Garnish with the parsley.

Globe artichokes are very popular in Mediterranean and Middle Eastern cooking. You can cook them whole and nibble the tender bases of each leaf, but it's the heart that has the tender, savoury flesh. I buy bottled marinated artichokes (not in water) and use them on antipasti platters, salads, on pizza, in paella, with lamb and blitzed into delicious dips.

All Purpose Mozambican Peri Peri Sauce

Ingredients:

- 1–10 African peri peri red chillies, roughly chopped
    - 1–3 chillies for a mild sauce
    - 4–6 chillies for a hot sauce
    - 7–10 chillies for a very hot sauce
- 8 cloves of garlic
- 1/2 red pepper
- 125ml (1/2 cup) freshly squeezed lemon juice
- 125ml (1/2 cup) white wine vinegar
- 1 tbsp light brown sugar
- 1 tbsp tomato paste
- 2 tsp chilli flakes
- 2 tsp dried oregano
- 2 tsp dried thyme
- 2 tsp salt
- 1 tsp paprika
- 1 tsp cayenne pepper
- 250ml (1 cup) olive oil

Makes 250ml

Method:

1. Wash a glass bottle in hot soapy water and dry it in the oven at 150°C for 10 minutes.
2. Place all the ingredients except the olive oil in a food processor and blitz until smooth and lump free.
3. Gradually pour in the olive oil and process until the oil has emulsified with the rest of the ingredients to form a sauce of pouring consistency.
4. Bottle the sauce immediately in the clean, sterilised bottle.
5. This will keep fresh in the fridge for up to 1 month. It can be used as a marinade, baste or condiment. Add extra lemon juice and fresh parsley and coriander when using.

African peri peri chillies, also known as African birds' eye chillies, are native to Mozambique. These chillies are used in the famously potent peri peri sauces (also known as piri piri or pil pil). You can grow your own chilli plant by ordering the seeds from www.sowchillies.co.uk or you can substitute Thai birds' eye chillies for a similar heat – or a milder chilli if you prefer.

Monica's Orange Mousse with Passionfruit Cream

Ingredients:

Orange mousse:
- 3 tbsp orange zest
- 3 tbsp caster sugar
- 150ml freshly squeezed orange juice
- 500ml single cream
- 2 egg whites

Passionfruit cream:
- 250ml cream
- 125ml (1/2 cup) lemon curd (see recipe below)
- pulp of 2 passionfruit

To serve:
- pulp of 1 passionfruit
- fresh raspberries
- mint leaves

Serves 8

Method:

1. To make the orange mousse, whisk together the orange zest, sugar and orange juice until the sugar dissolves.
2. In a separate bowl, whip the cream until soft peaks form. Gradually trickle in the orange syrup, whisking continuously until stiff.
3. In a clean, dry bowl, whisk the egg whites until stiff peaks form. Gently fold the egg whites into the whipped cream.
4. Divide the orange mousse between 8 glasses and allow to chill in the fridge while you make the passionfruit cream.
5. Whisk the cream and lemon curd until soft peaks form. Stir in the passionfruit pulp.
6. Spoon the passionfruit cream on top of the orange mousse. Garnish with extra passionfruit pulp, raspberries and fresh mint.

My cheat's lemon curd: in a bowl over a pot of simmering water, combine 1 tin of condensed milk, 2 egg yolks and the juice of 1 lemon. Stir for 5–7 minutes while the mixture thickens – it should be thick enough to coat the back of a spoon. Allow to cool before using.

Papaya Chilli Cooler

Ingredients:

- 4 slices papaya
- 1 small slice of red chilli
- 4 tbsp yoghurt
- 1 tbsp lime juice
- 1tbsp honey
- 25ml light rum
- 1/3 cup ice
- red chillies, to garnish

Serves 1

Method:

1. Mix the papaya, chilli slice, yoghurt, lime juice, honey, rum and ice in a blender until smooth and lump free.
2. Pour into a tall chilled glass and garnish with a red chilli.

Yerba Maté Watermelon Iced Tea

Ingredients:

- 1/4 cup dried yerba maté tea
- Juice and zest of 2 oranges
- 1 litre boiling water
- 1/2 honey
- 250g fresh watermelon
- ice cubes, to serve
- watermelon wedges, to serve
- extra orange zest, to serve

Serves 8

Method:

1. Pour the boiling water over the dried tea and orange zest. Allow to steep for 5 minutes.
2. Strain the tea and stir in the honey to dissolve.
3. Allow to cool for an hour, then transfer to the fridge to cool completely.
4. In a food processor, combine the watermelon, cold tea and orange juice. Blitz up till completely lump free.
5. Serve the iced tea over ice, with watermelon wedges and orange zest to garnish.

Chapter 7

Chinese*ish*

Moreish Asian Beef Skewers

Ingredients:

- 500g beef fillet or sirloin, diced into large pieces
- 4 tbsp flour seasoned with salt and pepper
- 3 spring onions, sliced
- 1 red chilli, sliced
- lemon wedges, to serve
- toasted sesame oil, to serve

Marinade paste:
- 2 cloves of garlic, sliced
- 1 stick of lemongrass, white part only, grated with a Microplane grater
- 1 spring onion, sliced
- 1 red chilli, sliced
- 1 thumb-sized piece of fresh ginger, grated
- 100ml plum sauce
- 2 tbsp soy sauce
- 1 tbsp sunflower oil

Serves 6

Method:

1. Soak 12 bamboo skewers in cold water for 1 hour.
2. Pulse together all the marinade paste ingredients in a blender.
3. Coat the diced beef well in the seasoned flour, then pat on half of the marinade paste. Thread the beef onto the skewers and grill on a hot BBQ for 3 minutes on each side. This will cook the meat to medium rare. If you prefer your beef well cooked, move the skewers to a medium-hot part of the grill and cook further.
4. Serve the skewers garnished with the sliced spring onions, red chillies and lemon wedges and a few drops of toasted sesame oil. Serve the rest of the marinade on the side as a dipping sauce.

Plum sauce is a thick sweet and sour sauce made from plums and other soft stone fruit such as peaches and apricots. You can make your own or use a shop-bought sauce straight from the bottle as a dipping sauce for spring rolls, dumplings and other Chinese nibbles. It's essential for marinades and stir-fry sauces in Chinese cooking.

Sticky Sweet 'n' Sour Chicken

Ingredients:

- 6 chicken pieces
- sunflower oil
- salt and freshly ground black pepper
- 2 red onions, cut into thick rings
- 2 red peppers, sliced into wide strips
- 2 yellow peppers, sliced into wide strips
- 1 x 400g tin of pineapple rings, drained and juice reserved

Sweet and sour sauce:
- 125ml (1/2 cup) rice wine vinegar
- 125ml (1/2 cup) chicken stock (use a corner of a stock cube)
- 4 tbsp tomato ketchup
- 4 tbsp plum sauce
- 4 tbsp light soy sauce
- 2 tbsp cornflour dissolved in 1 tbsp water
- reserved pineapple juice from the tin above

Serves 6

Method:

1. Put all the sauce ingredients in a small pot and mix well. Bring to the boil and bubble for 3–5 minutes, until it's shiny and glossy. Divide in half: one half for basting and one half to drizzle over the finished dish.
2. Lightly oil the chicken and season with salt and pepper. On a hot BBQ, grill each side of the chicken for 5–7 minutes, until crispy. Baste well with the sweet and sour sauce. Move the chicken to a medium part of the BBQ and cook each side for a further 10–12 minutes, basting with the sauce. Cut open the chicken at the thickest part and check that there's no pink and that it's cooked through.
3. Lightly oil the veggies and pineapple rings with sunflower oil and season with salt and pepper. Grill on a medium-hot BBQ until charred and softened. Set aside.
4. When the chicken is cooked through, serve with the grilled veggies and pineapple. Drizzle over the remaining sauce.

Light soy sauce, which is lighter in colour and consistency than dark soy sauce, is more widely used in cooking. Unless dark soy sauce is specified in a recipe, use light soy sauce. Light soy is saltier than dark soy sauce, so it should be used more sparingly. Ideal as a dipping sauce or condiment, light soy sauce is also preferable when you don't want the overall sauce to be dark in colour.

Succulent Pulled Pork Lettuce Cups

Ingredients:

- 3kg bone in pork shoulder

Spice rub:
- 4 tbsp Chinese 5 Spice
- 1 tsp freshly ground black pepper
- 1 tsp Szechuan peppercorns, crushed
- 1tbsp salt
- 1 thumb fresh ginger, peeled and grated
- 5 cloves garlic, crushed
- 2 tbsp soft brown sugar

Poaching liquid:
- 2 litres pomegranate juice
- juice of 4 limes
- 1 thumb ginger, peeled and sliced
- 2 whole star anise
- 1 red onion, roughly chopped
- 3 tbsp dark soy sauce
- 1 red chilli, roughly chopped

To serve:
- 6 baby gem or cos lettuces, leaves separated
- 3 fresh mangoes, peeled and sliced
- seeds of 1 pomegranate
- juice of 4 limes
- few dropped sesame oil
- 6 spring onions, finely sliced
- 2 tbsp black sesame seeds
- 4 tbsp coriander or micro salad leaves

Method:

1. Mix all the ingredients for the rub and rub into the meat, getting into every nook and cranny. Cover and refrigerate overnight.
2. Place the pork shoulder into a large roasting tin. Add all the ingredients for the poaching liquid and cover very well with tin foil, sealing it tightly.
3. Slow cook the pork shoulder at 140°C for 5 hours, basting regularly and turning over half way through.
4. Remove the pork shoulder from the oven dish and place onto a hot BBQ. Grill until crispy on all sides.
5. Skim the sauce from the baking tray then simmer until reduced to a thick syrup.
6. Slice or shred the pork with 2 forks. Pour over a little sauce. Serve the meat in a lettuce leaf mixed with mango and pomegranate and seasoned with lime juice and sesame oil. Garnish with coriander, sesame sesame seeds and spring onions.

Serves 4

Chinese 5 Spice is one of my favourite Pantry Pals. An aromatic blend of spices which include: star anise, cassia, ginger, Szechuan peppercorns, fennel seeds, cloves, white pepper, and cinnamon, depending on the blend. It is really easy to make your own blend, which you can store in an airtight container for up to 6 months.

Soy-glazed Salmon Burgers

Ingredients:

Asian aioli:
- 2 cloves of garlic, crushed
- 125ml (1/2 cup) mayonnaise
- juice of 1 lime
- 4 tbsp sour cream
- 2 tsp finely grated fresh ginger
- salt and freshly ground black pepper

Soy glaze:
- 1 tbsp cornflour
- 80ml dark soy sauce
- 3 tbsp honey
- 1 tbsp rice wine vinegar
- 1 tbsp sunflower oil

Salmon burgers:
- 2 spring onions, finely sliced
- 1 egg
- 65g (2/3 cup) fresh breadcrumbs
- 1 tbsp aioli
- 1 tsp hot chilli sauce
- salt and freshly ground black pepper
- 500g salmon fillets, finely chopped
- 4 sesame seed buns
- 1 cucumber, peeled into long ribbons
- 2 medium carrots, peeled into ribbons
- 50g pea shoots or micro salad

Serves 4

Method:

1. Mix together all the ingredients for the aioli, cover and refrigerate. Keep 1 tablespoon aside for the salmon burger mix.
2. To make the soy glaze, dissolve the cornflour in a little cold water until it's smooth and lump free. Pour all the glaze ingredients into a small pot and bring to the boil on top of the BBQ grill or on the hob. Boil the glaze for approximately 3 minutes, until it's thick, shiny and syrupy.
3. To make the salmon burgers, mix together the spring onions, egg, breadcrumbs, the reserved aioli and hot chilli sauce and season with salt and pepper. Add this to the chopped fresh salmon and mix gently. Form into 4 patties, cover and refrigerate for 20 minutes.
4. To cook the salmon burgers, heat a grill to a medium heat and lightly oil with sunflower oil to make it non-stick. Place the burgers on the grill and cook for 3 minutes, until lightly browned. Turn over and baste with the soy glaze. Cook for 3 more minutes and turn once more, glazing the other side. Cook for a further 4–5 minutes, brushing with the glaze, until just opaque.
5. Lightly toast the buns, then place a salmon burger on top and dress with the aioli, cucumber, carrot and pea shoots. Serve immediately.

Dark soy sauce is a staple condiment throughout Asia, made from fermented soybeans, roasted grains, water and salt. To give it a dark colour and thicker consistency, molasses is added and it's aged for longer. Dark soy sauce needs to be cooked to bring out its full flavour, so it's ideal for marinades, basting and glazes.

BBQ Sharing Platter of Ribs, Wings, Sausages, Cabbage, Squash and Mushrooms

Ingredients:

- 1kg pork ribs, cut into 2 rib pieces
- 1kg chicken wings
- 1kg cocktail pork sausages
- 1/2 butternut squash, the bulbous part sliced into wedges
- 8 large brown mushrooms
- 1 small purple cabbage, sliced into 8 wedges
- sunflower oil

Sticky marinade and basting sauce:
- 8 cloves of garlic, crushed
- 2 thumb-sized pieces of fresh ginger, grated
- 250g dark brown sugar
- 200g honey
- 250ml hoisin sauce
- 250ml pale dry sherry
- 200ml soy sauce
- 200ml sweet chilli sauce
- 50ml sunflower oil
- 2 tbsp Chinese five spice powder

Serves 8

Method:

1. Mix all the marinade ingredients together in a pot and simmer, covered, on a gentle heat for 10 minutes. Reserve 500ml (2 cups) of the sauce for basting.
2. Add the rib pieces to a large pot of boiling, salted water. Reduce to a vigorous simmer and cook for 10 minutes, then drain. Coat well in the marinade and set aside for 30 minutes. Place on a hot BBQ and grill for about 20 minutes, until sticky and delicious, basting just before serving.
3. Coat the chicken wings in 2 tablespoons of sunflower oil and grill on a hot BBQ for 10–12 minutes, until crispy. Remove from the heat and toss well in some of the marinade. Return to the grill and BBQ until the marinade caramelises. Coat with a little more sauce just before serving.
4. Coat the sausages in sunflower oil and grill on a medium BBQ for 5 minutes. Baste with the sticky sauce and grill on a medium-hot BBQ until caramelised and cooked through – these will only take 10–15 minutes.
5. Brush the butternut squash with a little of the sauce and grill on a medium-hot BBQ for 20–25 minutes, until softened and cooked through with nice grill marks.
6. Coat the mushrooms in a little of the sauce and grill on a medium-hot BBQ for 8–10 minutes, until softened and starting to wrinkle.
7. Brush the cabbage with sunflower oil and grill on a medium-hot BBQ until slightly charred and just tender in the middle. Brush on a little of the sauce and grill until the edges caramelise.

Hoisin sauce, also known as Chinese BBQ sauce, is a mixture of soy, garlic, spices and molasses. It has a unique flavour and is often mixed with other sauces to create the perfect stir-fry, marinade or dipping sauce.

Sticky Citrusy Prawn Salad

Ingredients:

- 20–25 large tiger prawns, shelled, headed and deveined
- 8 baby corn cobs, sliced
- 6 spring onions, finely sliced
- 2 carrots, peeled into ribbons
- 1/2 head of Chinese cabbage, finely shredded
- 100g bean sprouts
- 100g mangetout or sugar snap peas
- 2 tbsp sesame seeds, toasted

Marinade:
- 2 cloves of garlic, crushed
- 1 thumb-sized piece of fresh ginger, grated
- 1 x 10cm lemongrass stalk, grated with a Microplane grater
- 200ml freshly squeezed orange juice
- 100ml soy sauce
- juice of 2 lemons
- 2 tbsp balsamic vinegar
- 2 tbsp maple syrup
- 1 tbsp toasted sesame oil

Serves 4

Method:

1. Mix all the marinade ingredients together in a bowl, then add the prawns and marinate for 20 minutes in the fridge. Lift out the prawns and reserve the marinade.
2. Heat a griddle pan or BBQ and cook the prawns for 3–5 minutes, until they're pink, curled up and firm with nice griddle marks.
3. Put the marinade in a pan and place it on the heat. Let it bubble up until it turns thick and syrupy.
4. Mix all the vegetables with the cooked prawns and drizzle over the marinade. Garnish with toasted sesame seeds.

Toasted sesame oil is a deliciously nutty, amber-coloured oil that's widely used as a condiment in Asian cooking. It has quite an intense flavour, so I sprinkle a little over noodles, stir-fries and Asian salads. It's my secret ingredient in fried rice – I couldn't do without it.

Asian Mushroom, Pak Choi and Potato Salad

Ingredients:

- 500g baby potatoes, halved
- 400g mixed whole Asian mushrooms (oyster, shiitake and brown mushrooms), wiped clean
- sunflower oil
- salt and freshly ground black pepper
- 2 heads of pak choi, halved
- 50g alfalfa sprouts or micro salads
- handful of coriander, chopped

Dressing:
- 3 cloves of garlic, crushed
- 1 thumb-sized piece of fresh ginger, grated
- 100ml peanut oil
- juice of 2 limes
- 2 tbsp Shaoxing rice wine
- 2 tbsp soy sauce
- 1 tsp wholegrain mustard
- 1 tsp honey
- black or white pepper

Serves 6 as a side salad

Method:

1. Mix together all the dressing ingredients and season to taste with black or white pepper and allow to infuse. The soy sauce is salty, so you won't need to add salt.
2. Boil the halved baby potatoes for 12 minutes, until just tender. Drain well. If you want crispy potatoes, coat them in sunflower oil, season with salt and pepper and grill on a hot BBQ or under an oven grill.
3. Lightly coat the mushrooms in sunflower oil and season with salt and pepper. Grill on a hot BBQ for 5–6 minutes, until browned and cooked through. Transfer to a bowl, pour over half the dressing and allow to marinate; reserve the rest of the dressing for drizzling.
4. Lightly coat the pak choi with sunflower oil and season with salt and pepper. Grill on the hot BBQ for 3–5 minutes, until charred and slightly wilted. Break apart the leaves.
5. To serve, artistically arrange the potatoes, grilled mushrooms and pak choi on a platter. Scatter over the sprouts or micro salads and the coriander. Drizzle over the remaining dressing and serve warm.

Shaoxing rice wine plays a major role in Chinese cuisine, second only to soy sauce. Made from glutinous rice, it's used in marinades for meat, as it helps tenderise the meat, in sauces and even soups. It can be tricky to find in supermarkets so I often substitute a pale dry sherry, which works extremely well.

Crunchy Veg Noodle Salad

Ingredients:

- 250g ready-to-eat fresh egg noodles
- 1 red pepper, finely sliced
- 1 yellow pepper, finely sliced
- 1 red onion, very finely sliced
- 1 medium carrot, peeled into ribbons
- 75g mangetout or sugar snap peas
- 75g baby corn, halved
- 75g bean sprouts
- 30g roasted peanuts, roughly chopped

Dressing:
- 2 cloves of garlic, chopped
- 30g caster sugar
- 15g (1/2 cup) fresh basil
- 15g (1/2 cup) fresh coriander
- 10g (1/4 cup) fresh mint
- juice of 4 limes
- 1 tsp fish sauce
- 1 tsp soy sauce
- 50ml sunflower oil
- salt and freshly ground black pepper

Serves 6 as a side salad

Method:

1. Blitz all the dressing ingredients except the sunflower oil in a food processor. Once the dressing is a smooth paste, slowly drizzle in the oil to form an emulsion. Season with salt and pepper and allow to infuse.
2. Break up the fresh egg noodles and mix with the veggies in a large bowl. Drizzle over the dressing and toss through. Garnish with roasted peanuts.

Chinese noodles were first documented in 22 AD. They are an integral part of Chinese cuisine and culture. There are a vast variety of noodles produced, varying in ingredients, size, shape and according to region. My favourite noodles are fresh egg noodles, but the vacuum-packed ready-to-eat noodles are a great Pantry Pal. They can be used in salads, soups and stir-fries to add substance and texture.

Beetroot Sesame Citrus Salad

Ingredients:

- 4 fresh beetroot
- 1 tbsp sunflower oil
- salt and freshly ground black pepper
- 2 tsp sesame seeds
- 150g red lettuce leaves (lollo rosso, radicchio, red oak leaf)
- 3 oranges, zested and segmented
- 50g alfalfa sprouts or micro salads
- large bunch of coriander, chopped

Zesty dressing:
- juice and zest of 1/2 orange
- 2 tbsp soy sauce
- 4 tsp toasted sesame oil
- 2 tsp honey
- black or white pepper

Serves 6 as a side salad

Method:

1. Mix all the dressing ingredients together, season to taste with black or white pepper and allow to infuse.
2. Peel the beetroot and cut each one into 6–8 wedges, depending on their size – you still want to see the shape of the beetroot. Coat the wedges in the sunflower oil and season with salt and pepper. Grill on a medium-hot BBQ for about 30 minutes, until cooked through, or roast in the oven at 190°C on a baking tray for 30 minutes, until crispy and cooked through.
3. Lightly toast the sesame seeds in a clean, dry pan until they start to pop.
4. Arrange the lettuce leaves, orange segments and roasted beetroot on a platter. Scatter over the alfalfa sprouts or micro salad leaves, toasted sesame seeds, orange zest and fresh coriander.
5. Drizzle over a little of the dressing just before serving.

Sesame seeds add a nutty taste and a delicate, subtle crunch to many Asian dishes. You can get several different types of sesame seeds, ranging in colour from cream to red through to black. Buy small bags of sesame seeds and store them in a jar or small plastic container in the freezer to keep them fresh. Lightly toast them in a dry pan until they pop to bring out the flavour.

Lychee Jam Jar Cheesecake

Ingredients:

- 500g cream cheese, at room temperature
- 250ml shop-bought lemon curd
- 300ml cream, stiffly whipped
- 2 x 400g tins of lychees or 500g fresh lychees, peeled and pitted
- 1 x 135g packet of orange or lemon jelly, dissolved according to packet instructions

Base:
- 150g ginger nut biscuits
- 60g butter, melted

Serves 6

Method:

1. Leave the cream cheese out at room temperature for 1 hour.
2. Meanwhile, to make the base, crush the biscuits in a ziplock bag with a rolling pin. Mix the melted butter with the crushed biscuits in a bowl. Divide equally between 6 jam jars and compress lightly. Chill in the fridge for at least 30 minutes.
3. To make the cheesecake layer, whisk the lemon curd into the softened cream cheese until it's smooth, creamy and lump free, then fold in the whipped cream.
4. Roughly chop one-third of the lychees and mix them through the cheesecake filling. Divide the filling equally between the jam jars and smooth the surface. Chill in the fridge.
5. Divide the remaining lychees between the jam jars. Pour over the dissolved jelly and chill in the fridge until it's set.

Lychees are a sweet, floral-scented fruit native to China. Rambutan are a similar-tasting, but hairy-looking, version of the brown-skinned lychee. Ideally used fresh to preserve the delicate aromatic scent, canned lychees are still delicious and very versatile. Add the fruit and syrup of tinned lychees to an ordinary fruit salad to transform it, or simply use them with ice cream or in cocktails.

Watermelon and Star Anise Relish

Ingredients:

- 1 vanilla bean
- 2 star anise
- 100ml palm sugar or light brown sugar (use your measuring jug to measure by volume)
- juice of 1 lime
- 2 tbsp rice wine vinegar
- pinch of sea salt
- 2 shallots, very thinly sliced
- 400g watermelon, scooped into balls
- 200g baby rosa or baby plum tomatoes, halved

Makes 2 large jars

Method:

1. Remove the rubber seal from 2 large Kilner jars and wash the jars in hot soapy water. Rinse very well in clean water and place upside on the oven shelf. Bake for 10 minutes at 150°C to dry and sterilise the jars.
2. Halve the vanilla bean and scoop the vanilla seeds into a pot (keep the halves). Add the star anise, sugar, 100ml water, lime juice, rice wine vinegar and salt. Gently heat to dissolve the sugar.
3. Add the shallots, watermelon and tomatoes and gently heat – do not overcook or it will turn to mush.
4. Bottle the relish immediately while it's still hot, dividing it between the 2 jars (make sure each jar gets 1 star anise). Insert half a vanilla bean into each jar.
5. Store in the fridge for 5–7 days. Delicious served with barbecued meats, especially pork.

Star anise is a woody, liquorice-scented, star-shaped pod filled with seeds that's native to China. Star anise is widely used in Chinese and Vietnamese cooking and is a secret ingredient in some Indian dishes. It's also a key spice in Chinese five spice powder. Look out for unbroken star anise when purchasing them and use them whole in cooking.

Lychee and Ginger Martini

Ingredients:

- 25ml vodka
- 25ml lychee liqueur
- 2 slices of fresh ginger
- 100ml fresh lychee juice
- Fresh lychees, to garnish

Serves 1

Method:

1. Place all the ingredients in a cocktail shaker with ice and give it a good shake.
2. Using a strainer, strain the martini into a chilled martini glass.
3. Garnish with lychees.

Very Berry Green Iced Tea

Ingredients:

- 4 green tea teabags or 4tbsp of loose green tea
- 1 thumb ginger, peeled and sliced
- 1 litre boiling water
- 1/2 cup honey
- 250g raspberries, frozen
- 250g bluberries, frozen
- 250g fresh strawberries, sliced

Serves 8

Method:

1. Pour the boiling water over the tea and sliced ginger. Leave to infuse for 5 minutes.
2. Remove the tea bags and ginger or strain if using loose tea. Stir in the honey to dissolve.
3. Allow to cool for an hour then transfer to the fridge to cool completely.
4. Serve with frozen blueberries and raspberries and fresh strawberries.

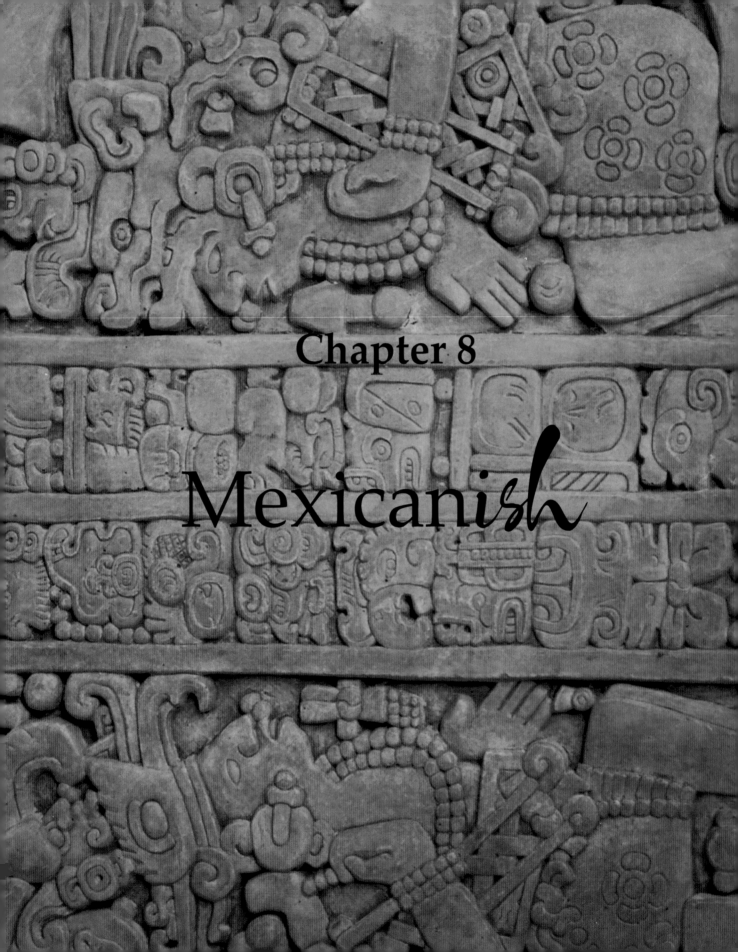

Chapter 8

Mexican*ish*

Spicy Tuna Steak with Peppadew Papaya Salad

Ingredients:

- 4 thick tuna steaks
- salt and freshly ground black pepper
- 2 limes, halved

Spicy marinade:
- 125ml (1/2 cup) tomato paste
- juice of 3 limes
- small bunch of fresh coriander stalks
- 2 tbsp sunflower oil
- 1 tbsp ground cumin
- 1 tbsp ground coriander
- 1 tbsp agave syrup or honey
- 2 tsp chilli powder

Peppadew papaya salad:
- 1 x 400g tin of black beans, rinsed and drained
- 1 x 200g tin of sweetcorn, rinsed and drained
- 1 papaya, peeled and cubed
- 1/2 small red onion, finely diced
- 250g cherry tomatoes, halved
- 2 tbsp chopped peppadews
- zest and juice of 2 limes
- 1 ripe avocado, diced
- 15g (1/2 cup) chopped fresh coriander
- salt and freshly ground black pepper

Serves 4 as a main course

Method:

1. Mix all the marinade ingredients together and reserve 2 tablespoons for basting. Cover the tuna steak with the marinade and leave for 20 minutes.
2. Scrape the marinade off the tuna steaks and season well with salt and pepper. Place on a very hot BBQ and grill for 2–3 minutes on each side, basting both sides with the reserved marinade. Squeeze over half a lime on each tuna steak while grilling. Tuna steak is best served pink, so don't overcook it.
3. To make the peppadew papaya salad, mix together the black beans, sweetcorn, papaya, red onion, cherry tomatoes and peppadews in a bowl. In a separate bowl, squeeze the lime juice and zest over the avocado, then add to the salad along with the fresh coriander. Check the seasoning and season well with salt and pepper.
4. Cut the tuna steaks in half so that you can see the juicy pink inside and serve with the peppadew papaya salad.

Agave syrup is the sweet golden syrup extracted from several cactus varieties that are related to the tequila cactus. The syrup has a thinner consistency than honey and a more neutral taste, so it's ideal for adding sweetness without the distinctive taste of honey. Agave syrup ranges from pale gold to dark amber in colour – I prefer the dark agave syrup, as it's unfiltered and so retains more of the plants' natural minerals.

Smoky BBQ Steak Skewers with Mexican Chimichurri Salsa

Ingredients:

- 2 x thick 700g sirloin or rump steaks, diced into large chunks
- 2 red peppers, cut into chunks
- 2 yellow peppers, cut into chunks
- 2 cloves of garlic, crushed
- 4 tbsp olive oil
- 2 tbsp Worcestershire sauce
- 1 tbsp tomato ketchup
- 1 tbsp soy sauce
- 1 tsp dried oregano
- 1 tsp smoked paprika
- smoked sea salt and freshly ground black pepper

Chimichurri salsa:
- 3 tomatoes, skinned, seeded and diced
- 3 cloves of garlic, crushed
- 2 bay leaves
- 1 red onion, finely chopped
- 100ml olive oil
- 80ml red wine vinegar
- 60ml soy sauce
- 4 tbsp chopped fresh flat-leaf parsley
- 2 tbsp chopped fresh oregano
- 1 tbsp dried oregano
- 1 tsp chilli flakes
- 1 tsp paprika
- 1 tsp ground cumin

Serves 4–6

Method:

1. Soak 12 bamboo skewers in cold water for 1 hour (or use metal skewers).
2. In a large bowl, mix together the steak pieces, peppers, garlic, olive oil, Worcestershire sauce, tomato ketchup, soy sauce, oregano, smoked paprika and plenty of smoked salt and pepper. Marinate for 1 hour.
3. Meanwhile, to make the chimichurri salsa, mix all the ingredients together in a bowl and set aside to infuse. Remove the bay leaves before serving.
4. Thread the meat and peppers onto the skewers, alternating meat with peppers. Place the skewers on a hot BBQ and grill for 15–20 minutes, until done to your liking.
5. Serve the steak skewers hot with dollops of chimichurri.

Smoked sea salt is a really useful gourmet Pantry Pal. The best smoked sea salts are made using large crystals of natural sea salt that are smoked in a specialised smoker using burning wood chips to create aromatic smoke that clings to and permeates the salt. Different varieties of wood can be used to achieve different flavours in the salt.

Tremaine's Sticky Spicy Chutney Chicken

Ingredients:

- 8 chicken pieces (drumsticks and thighs)
- 2 tbsp sunflower oil
- salt and freshly ground black pepper

Sticky spicy chutney baste:
- 2 cloves of garlic, crushed
- 250ml (1 cup) tomato paste
- 250ml (1 cup) peach or mango chutney
- 50ml (1/4 cup) red wine vinegar
- 2 tbsp dark brown sugar
- 1 tbsp ground coriander
- 1 tbsp ground cumin
- 2 tsp chipotle paste
- salt and freshly ground black pepper

Pineapple salsa:
- 1 medium pineapple, diced, or 1 large tin of pineapple chunks
- 1/2 red onion, finely diced
- 1/2 red chilli, finely chopped
- juice of 2 limes
- 2 tbsp chopped fresh coriander

Serves 4 as a main course

Method:

1. Mix all the baste ingredients together in a bowl and set aside.
2. Oil the chicken pieces with the sunflower oil and season with salt and pepper.
3. On a hot grill, seal both sides of the chicken for 5–6 minutes, until charred and crispy, then baste well with the sauce.
   Move to a medium-hot part of the BBQ and cook for a further 10–15 minutes on each side and baste with the sauce. Chicken pieces on the bone take approximately 35–45 minutes to cook like this. Insert a knife in the thickest part to check that there is no pink and that the juice runs clear.
4. To make the salsa, mix together the pineapple, red onion, chilli and lime juice in a bowl and allow the flavours to infuse for 10 minutes. Add the coriander just before serving.
5. Serve the sticky chicken hot with pineapple salsa. It's also delicious cold – shred the meat and stuff it into a pita pocket with salsa and crunchy lettuce.

Chipotle paste is made from fully ripened red jalapeño peppers that are dried and smoked. This can be turned into a paste or sauce and added to grilled meats, fish and bean dishes. This distinctive smoky, hot flavour is integral to Mexican cooking and can really transform a boring dish into something special. It's available at good speciality stores or you can try making your own.

Smoked Paprika BBQ Pork Chops with Guava Salsa

Ingredients:

- 4 thick pork chops, fat scored so that it doesn't curl up
- salt and freshly ground black pepper
- lime wedges, to serve

Marinade:
- 2 cloves of garlic, crushed
- 125ml (1/2 cup) tomato ketchup
- zest and juice of 1 orange
- 5 tbsp fresh oregano leaves or 2 tbsp dried oregano
- 3 tbsp red wine vinegar
- 1 tbsp smoked paprika

Guava salsa:
- 4–6 guava, diced (tinned is fine)
- 1 small fresh papaya, peeled and diced
- 1/2 cucumber, diced
- 1/2 red onion, finely diced
- juice of 2 limes
- salt and freshly ground black pepper
- 4 tbsp chopped fresh coriander

Serves 4

Method:

1. Combine all the ingredients for the marinade in a large dish. Reserve 4 tablespoons for basting. Immerse the pork chops in the marinade, cover and refrigerate overnight.
2. Mix together all the guava salsa ingredients except the coriander and season to taste. Leave to infuse.
3. Scrape the marinade off the pork chops, then season the chops with salt and pepper. Grill on a medium-hot BBQ for 4 minutes per side, until sealed. Don't forget to turn the chops onto the fatty side to crisp it up.
4. Using a silicone brush, baste the pork chops with the reserved marinade and grill for a further 5–10 minutes per side. Pork chops will take 15–20 minutes to cook through on a medium grill, depending on how thick they are. Check that the fattest part of the meat is opaque and cooked through.
5. Baste the meat again when it comes off the grill and just before serving for extra flavour and juiciness.
6. Add the coriander to the salsa and serve with the pork chops, with lime wedges on the side.

Guavas are a wonderful firm fruit that are native to Mexico. There are several different varieties, from white fleshed, through to pink and red in colour. Delicious raw in salads and savoury dishes, guavas can also be poached and served with custard for dessert. Guavas make a refreshing fruit juice and excellent jam and liqueurs. Tinned guavas are delicious and are an excellent substitute for the fresh fruit.

Norman's Enamel Mug Eggs

Ingredients:

- 100g chorizo sausage, finely diced
- 100g cherry tomatoes, halved
- 1/2 red onion, finely diced
- 4 eggs
- crème fraîche, to serve
- pinch of paprika
- 2 tbsp chopped fresh flat-leaf parsley
- salt and freshly ground black pepper

Cheesy dipping toast:
- 4–6 thick slices of sourdough or ciabatta bread
- butter or olive oil, for frying
- 100g grated Parmesan cheese

Serves 4

Method:

1. Divide the chorizo, cherry tomatoes and red onion between 4 enamel mugs. Crack an egg into each mug. Place a deep skillet or saucepan on the grill of a medium-hot BBQ and put the mugs inside. Pour boiling water into the skillet or pan until it comes one-third of the way up the mugs. The eggs are done when the egg white is cooked – give the mugs a jiggle to see how set they are.
2. To make the cheesy dipping toast, cut the bread into thick fingers. Spread with butter or drizzle over a little olive oil. Spread the grated cheese over a chopping board or plate and roll the bread in it. Fry the bread in batches in a little oil in a frying pan until golden and crispy. Drain on kitchen paper before serving.
3. Serve the eggs hot with a dollop of crème fraîche, a pinch of paprika, parsley, salt and pepper and the cheesy dipping toast.

I absolutely adore chorizo, the cured Spanish pork sausage seasoned with paprika, chilli and garlic. Mexican chorizo is traditionally raw, and it's ideal cooked straight on the BBQ. I buy the fully cured Spanish chorizo and use it to flavour dishes with its wonderful spicy smokiness. Fry up a little chorizo and use the wonderful paprika oil that comes out to fry onions, flavour egg dishes and jazz up beans. I wrap and freeze 100g pieces of chorizo – one of my essential Freezer Treasures.

Biltong Nachos with Strawberry Avocado Salsa

Ingredients:

- 1 large bag of corn tortilla chips
- 250g ricotta cheese
- 250g sliced biltong or Parma ham
- 2 red chillies, finely sliced
- 100g (1 cup) grated Pecorino cheese

Strawberry avocado salsa:
- juice of 2 limes
- 2 ripe avocados, peeled and diced
- 250g strawberries, finely sliced
- 1 tsp finely chopped jalapeño chillies
- salt and freshly ground black pepper
- 2 tbsp chopped fresh coriander

Serves 4

Method:

1. To make the salsa, squeeze the juice of 1 lime over the avocados to prevent discolouration. Gently mix together the avocados, strawberries, chillies and the rest of the lime juice. Season well with salt and pepper. Just before serving, stir through the coriander.
2. Arrange a layer of tortilla chips in a large skillet. Top with half the ricotta, half the biltong and half the salsa. Scatter half the chillies on top.
3. Layer the remaining chips, ricotta, biltong, salsa and the rest of the chillies. Sprinkle over the Pecorino cheese.
4. Place the skillet on a hot grill and cover it (I use a metal baking sheet if I don't have a lid). Grill for about 15 minutes, until the cheese has melted. Alternatively, you can bake the nachos on a baking tray in the oven at 180°C until golden and bubbling.
5. Serve the nachos hot with a cold beer.

Biltong is a traditionally spiced and cured meat from South Africa. It can be made from beef or venison, like springbuck or kudu. Top-quality cuts of meat are cured, spiced and dried. Biltong is sold as whole fillets or thinly sliced. Deliciously salty and spicy, biltong makes a great savoury snack and is a good source of lean protein.

BBQ Toasted Cheesy Chorizo Quesadillas

Ingredients:

- 8 tbsp sweet pepper or chilli relish
- 16 corn or flour tortillas
- 24–30 thin slices of chorizo sausage
- 8–10 jalapeño chillies or 1 red pepper, finely diced
- 8 spring onions, finely sliced
- 250g Manchego or mature Cheddar, grated
- Chilli and Orange Guacamole (see page 205), to serve

Serves 4

Method:

1. Spread a thin layer of relish on the tortillas. Arrange a single layer of chorizo slices on top of the relish. Add some chopped peppers and finely sliced spring onions, then sprinkle on a generous amount of grated cheese. Place another tortilla on top, then press down to compact the filling.
2. Place the quesadilla on a low to medium-hot BBQ (these also cook well on a griddle pan). Grill until the bottom tortilla begins to toast, keeping an eye on it so that you don't burn it. When the cheese starts to melt, turn the whole quesadilla over and cook the other side.
3. Cut into wedges and serve with Chilli and Orange Guacamole.

Tortillas are an essential Pantry Pal, especially if you have to pack lunchboxes or are watching your weight (no need for butter). They make great wraps and the quickest, low-fat toasted sandwiches ever. I favour corn or whole wheat tortillas for extra texture and fibre. Wrap well in cling film and freeze in twos or fours. They're also great as a vehicle for leftovers, a quick lunch or dinner with salad.

Cheesy Chilli BBQ Sweetcorn

Ingredients:

- 8 mielies (corn on the cob), preferably still with the leaves
- 100g butter, melted
- salt and freshly ground black pepper
- 8 tbsp mayonnaise
- 2 tsp chilli flakes
- 200g Parmesan cheese, finely grated

Serves 8

Method:

1. Pull back the leaves on the mielies and remove the fine fronds, but leave the green leaves on, like a tassle. Coat well in melted butter and season with salt and pepper. Grill on a medium BBQ until the corn is charred and softened.
2. Smear a layer of mayonnaise over each mielie until well coated, then sprinkle over some chilli flakes.
3. Spread the grated Parmesan cheese on a wooden board or plate. Roll the mielies in the cheese to coat well. Place the mielies back on the grill and toast until the cheese is golden.
4. Remove from the grill and sprinkle over a little more Parmesan and chilli flakes to taste.

Chilli flakes are an essential Pantry Pal not just in Mexican cooking, but a variety of cuisines. They're made from drying a variety of chillies and crumbling them up. Your eyes should water when you open a jar of top-quality chilli flakes. Chilli flakes also use the seeds, which are the hottest part, so a little goes a long way. I prefer loose chilli flakes, as a grinder with chilli flakes is more for use as a table seasoning.

Mexican Watermelon, Corn and Bean Salad

Ingredients:

- 1 x 400g tin of black beans or kidney beans, rinsed and drained
- 1 x 200g tin of sweetcorn, drained
- 6 peppadew peppers, sliced into thin strips
- 1 small red onion, finely sliced
- 750g diced watermelon
- 6 tbsp chopped fresh coriander

Dressing:
- 1 clove of garlic, minced
- juice of 2 limes
- 2 tbsp avocado oil
- 1 tsp ground cumin
- 1/2 tsp chilli flakes
- salt and freshly ground black pepper

Serves 6

Method:

1. Whisk together all the dressing ingredients and season well with salt and pepper.
2. Mix together the beans, sweetcorn, peppadews and red onion in a bowl. Pour over the dressing, cover and refrigerate for 1 hour to allow the flavours to infuse.
3. Just before serving, add the watermelon and fresh coriander.

Black beans and kidney beans are essential Pantry Pals for Mexican cooking. You can cook them from scratch or use tinned beans. Soak dried beans overnight, then discard the water, top up with fresh water and boil for 30 minutes. Change the water again and simmer until just tender. Boiling is important for kidney beans, as undercooked kidney beans are hazardous. These beans can be added to chillis, salads, taco fillings and even Mexican breakfast dishes.

Chilli and Orange Guacamole

Ingredients:

- 2 ripe avocados
- 1 small red chilli, seeded and finely chopped
- zest and juice of 1 orange
- 4 tbsp chopped fresh coriander
- salt and freshly ground black pepper

Makes 1 bowl

Method:

1. Mash the avocados in a bowl. Add the chilli, orange zest and juice and the fresh coriander (keep back a little of the chilli and orange zest for garnish). Season well with salt and pepper and garnish with a little chilli and orange zest.
2. Serve with nachos, grilled chicken or fish.

Tortilla chips are great to keep stashed away, ready for a party dip or snack. Make your own by taking a stack of flour tortillas and cutting each one into 8 wedges. Spread these out on a baking tray, making sure they don't overlap. Spray with a sunflower or olive oil spray and season with salt, cumin and chilli powder. Bake at 180°C for 5 minutes. Give the tray a shake and bake for a further 5 minutes, until just starting to colour. Ideally, serve warm with guacamole and salsa.

Norman's Chilli Rum Bananas with Ice Cream

Ingredients:

- 125g butter
- 125g dark brown sugar
- juice of 2 lemons
- 2 tsp vanilla extract
- 6 bananas, sliced
- 100ml dark rum
- 1.5 litres vanilla ice cream
- 4 tbsp desiccated coconut, lightly toasted, to decorate
- 1 tsp chilli flakes, to decorate

Makes 1 large jar

Method:

1. Heat the butter, brown sugar, 100ml water, lemon juice and vanilla extract in a pot until hot and bubbling. You can do this on the hob or on the BBQ. Add the bananas to the bubbling butter sugar and cook for 1–2 minutes to caramelise.
2. Remove the pot from the heat to add the rum, then return to the heat to burn off some of the alcohol. If the pot gets hot enough, the alcohol will ignite and you'll see a blue flame. If this doesn't happen, you can ignite it with a long safety match or a safety lighter. After a minute or two, kill the flame by putting on the lid or sliding a metal tray over the pot (this cuts off the oxygen).
3. Serve scoops of vanilla ice cream to each guest with a generous helping of rum banana on top. Decorate with a sprinkle of desiccated coconut and chilli flakes.

Dark rum is the dark amber spirit made from sugarcane and matured in oak barrels for a richer, more caramel flavour. Used in some cocktails, I also find rum indispensable to jazz up a fruit dessert and to soak dried fruit in for fruitcakes, Christmas puddings and compotes. Some traditional Caribbean recipes like jerk chicken also require a good dark rum, so you'll get good use out of it.

Strawberry Ginger Mojito

Ingredients:

- 4 strawberries, puréed
- juice of 1/2 lime
- 1 slice fresh ginger
- 4 mint leaves
- 1 tbsp sugar
- 50ml light rum
- 50ml soda water
- ginger slices, to garnish

Serves 1

Method:

1. Mix the strawberry purée with the lime juice, ginger, mint leaves, sugar and rum in a shaker. Muddle to release the flavours of the mint and ginger.
2. Add a scoop of ice and mix well.
3. Strain and pour into a tall chilled glass, top up with soda water.
4. Garnish with fresh ginger slices.

Hibiscus Lime Iced Tea

Ingredients:

- 1/4 cup dried hibiscus flowers
- 1/2 cup agavé syrup
- 1 litre boiling water
- 125ml lime juice
- ice cubes, to serve
- hibiscus flowers in syrup, to serve (optional)

Serves 8

Method:

1. Pour the boiling water over the hibiscus flowers and allow to infuse for 5 minutes.
2. Strain and stir through the agavé syrup.
3. Stir in the lime juice and allow to cool for an hour. Transfer to the fridge until completely chilled.
4. Serve over ice with 1 hibiscus flower in syrup per glass as garnish.

Chapter 9

Greekish

Andre's Pomegranate Glazed Lamb with Figs and Mint

Ingredients:

- 12 thickly sliced lamb chops
- 2 cloves of garlic, crushed
- 4 tbsp olive oil
- 4 tbsp pomegranate molasses
- juice of 1/2 lemon
- 2 sprigs of fresh rosemary
- salt and freshly ground black pepper

Sticky figs:
- 1 tbsp pomegranate molasses
- 1/2 tbsp extra virgin olive oil
- juice of 1/2 lemon
- salt and freshly ground black pepper
- 12 fresh figs, halved
- 200g creamy feta cheese
- 75g pistachios, toasted
- 2 tbsp finely chopped fresh mint

Serves 4 as a main dish

Method:

1. Score the fat all around the lamb chops with a sharp knife. This will prevent them from curling up when you grill them and also ensures a crispier finish.
2. Mix the garlic, olive oil, pomegranate molasses and lemon juice in a small bowl. Keep 1 tablespoon aside for basting. Coat the lamb chops in the pomegranate marinade. Rub the rosemary sprigs between your hands to release the oils, then tuck the sprigs around the lamb. Leave to marinate for 2–4 hours in the fridge.
3. Lift the lamb chops out of the marinade and scrape off any excess, or it will burn. Season the chops well with salt and freshly ground black pepper.
4. Grill the lamb chops on a hot BBQ for 4–5 minutes on each side for medium rare. Turn the chops with your tongs onto the fatty side for crispy fat. Brush the reserved marinade over for a sticky glaze and allow the lamb chops to rest, loosely wrapped in foil, for 5 minutes. Place 3 cutlets on each plate or a large platter or wooden board.
5. Mix together the pomegranate molasses, olive oil, lemon juice and some salt and pepper. Arrange the halved figs on the plates and crumble over the feta cheese. Drizzle over a little of the pomegranate syrup, then scatter over the toasted pistachios and finely chopped mint. Serve immediately.

Pomegranate molasses is traditionally used in Persian and Turkish cuisine and is one of my favourite Pantry Pals. Don't despair if you can't find it – you can easily make your own by combining 2 litres of pomegranate juice (from a carton), 250ml (1 cup) sugar and 125ml (1/2 cup) lemon juice in a pot. Bring to the boil, stirring. Reduce to a simmer and bubble away till you get a thick, glossy syrup.

Quinoa-stuffed Baby Calamari

Ingredients:

- 12 baby squid
- salt and freshly ground black pepper
- light olive oil
- lemon wedges, to serve
- Greek salad (see p. 227), to serve

Quinoa stuffing:
- 2 tbsp olive oil
- 1 red onion, diced
- 1 small red chilli, seeded and finely chopped
- 2 cloves of garlic, crushed
- 250ml (1 cup) quinoa
- 500ml (2 cups) chicken stock
- zest and juice of 1 lemon
- 1 tsp dried oregano
- 2 fresh tomatoes, skinned and finely diced
- 2 tbsp pitted Kalamata olives
- 2 tbsp chopped fresh flat-leaf parsley
- salt and freshly ground black pepper

Black Olive Chilli Tapenade:
- 1 clove garlic, crushed
- juice of 1 lemon
- 3 tbsp capers, chopped
- 6 anchovy fillets, chopped
- 250g black olives, pitted and roughly chopped
- 1tbsp flat-leaf parsley, chopped
- 1 red chilli, finely sliced
- 3 tbsp extra virgin olive oil
- freshly ground black pepper

Method:

1. Mix together the ingredients for the tapenade and leave to infuse, the texture should be quite coarse.
2. To make the quinoa stuffing, heat the olive oil in a non-stick frying pan over a medium heat. Gently fry the onion and chilli for 10 minutes, until very soft. Add the garlic and cook for a further 2 minutes. Add the quinoa, chicken stock, lemon zest and juice and oregano. Bring to the boil, then reduce to a simmer for 15–20 minutes, until the quinoa is coming apart and the liquid has evaporated. Stir in the diced tomatoes, olives and parsley. Season well with salt and pepper.
3. To prepare the baby squid, remove the tentacles and set aside. Squeeze out all the contents and remove the cartilage 'quill'. Rinse the tube very well under cold running water. Peel or scrape off the purple-pink membrane – this is tough and will contract and cause the squid tube to lose its shape.
4. Season the squid tube inside and out with salt and pepper. Brush the tentacles with light olive oil and season them too. Stuff the squid with the quinoa stuffing while it's still hot. Lightly score 3 diagonal lines on each side of the squid tube.
5. On a hot BBQ, grill the stuffed squid tubes for 4–5 minutes on each side, until they're white and opaque. Do not overcook! The tentacles should curl up and turn slightly crispy.
6. Serve with extra lemon wedges, salad leaves and black olive chilli tapenade.

Serves 6

Squid and octopus are much-loved dishes in Greek cuisine. It can be tricky to get fresh squid, depending on where you live, so I often buy frozen squid from my fishmonger or Asian market. You can get the large tubes, but I favour baby squid, as they tend to be more tender. To defrost them, place them in a colander and run cold water over them, washing off the ice. If you separate them and rinse them well, this should only take 20 minutes.

Marinated Goat Kebabs and Grilled Grapes

Ingredients:

- 2kg young goat meat or lamb, cut into large cubes
- 4 tbsp olive oil
- 2kg red seedless grapes, broken into fist-sized bunches
- 30 bamboo skewers, soaked in cold water for 1 hour

Marinade:
- 4 cloves of garlic, crushed
- 100ml light olive oil
- juice and zest of 2 lemons
- 6 tbsp finely chopped fresh oregano or 2 tbsp dried oregano
- 3 tbsp finely chopped fresh mint
- 3 tbsp ground cumin
- 3 tbsp honey
- 2 tbsp finely chopped fresh flat-leaf parsley
- 1 tbsp ground cinnamon
- salt and freshly ground black pepper

Minty tzatziki:
- 500g Greek yoghurt
- 1 large cucumber, peeled, seeded and grated
- 2 cloves of garlic, crushed
- juice of 1/2 lemon
- 2 tbsp finely chopped fresh mint
- 1 tsp salt
- 1/2 tsp ground white pepper

Serves 8 as a starter

Method:

1. Mix all the marinade ingredients together in a large bowl or container. Add the meat and mix well. Cover and marinate for at least 3 hours or up to 24 hours.
2. To make the minty tzatziki, place the yoghurt in a fine mesh sieve set over a bowl and drain for 3–4 hours. Wrap the cucumber in a clean tea towel and squeeze out the moisture. Transfer the drained yoghurt to a fresh bowl and add the cucumber, garlic, lemon juice, fresh mint and salt and white pepper. Stir to combine. Chill for 1–2 hours before serving.
3. Skewer the meat onto the bamboo skewers, pushing the pieces together tightly. Spread out the kebabs on a hot grill. Grill for 5 minutes, until well sealed, then turn over to seal the other side for 5 minutes. Turn again if you've missed any bits of meat sticking out. Continue to grill the kebabs for 15–20 minutes, until just cooked and tender. Remove from the grill and allow to rest for 5 minutes loosely covered in foil.
4. For the grilled grapes, pour the olive oil in a large bowl and add the grape bunches. Gently move the grapes around until they're covered in the oil. Grill the grape bunches on a medium BBQ until the grapes are warm and starting to burst slightly.
5. Serve the warm goat kebabs with the grilled grapes and tzatziki.

Ground cinnamon is widely used in Greek cooking, especially in marinades for meat and chicken. You may think of this spice as sweet and only suitable for desserts, but it really rounds out the flavours in meat dishes and softens gaminess. There's a huge difference in the quality and pungency of ground cinnamon, so check out local ethnic stores and speciality shops.

Greek Baked Beans on Toast

Ingredients:

- 2 tbsp olive oil
- 1 red onion, finely diced
- 2 cloves of garlic, crushed
- 150ml red wine
- 2 x 400g tins chopped tomatoes
- 2 tbsp tomato paste
- 2 tbsp fresh oregano or 1 tsp dried
- 1 tbsp brown sugar
- salt and freshly ground black pepper
- 1 x 400g tin butterbeans, rinsed and drained
- 250g baby spinach
- 1 loaf of crusty rustic bread, sliced
- 100g feta cheese, crumbled
- 2 tbsp chopped fresh flat-leaf parsley
- zest of 1 lemon

Serves 6 as a starter or snack

Method:

1. Heat the olive oil in a large pan over a medium heat. Gently sauté the onion for 10 minutes, until very soft. Add the garlic and cook for a further 2–3 minutes. Pour in the wine and let it bubble up until it has reduced by half. Add in the chopped tomatoes, tomato paste, oregano and brown sugar. Season well with salt and pepper and stir. Bring up to the boil, then lower the heat and simmer for 30 minutes, until thick and rich.
2. Add the rinsed and drained butterbeans and cook for a further 10 minutes. Stir in handfuls of the baby spinach and continue to cook until it wilts into the butterbeans.
3. Toast slices of bread on the BBQ. Transfer to a plate and add generous dollops of the butterbeans. Garnish with crumbled feta cheese, parsley and lemon zest. Serve hot or cold as a snack.

Oregano is one the most predominant herbs in Greek cooking. Greek oregano has a particularly pungent flavour and the name literally means 'joy in the mountain' in Greek. There are several types of oregano that are widely grown. The good news is that oregano dries very successfully, retaining much of its flavour, so make this herb your new Greek Pantry Pal.

Grilled Halloumi and Watermelon Salad

Ingredients:

- 200g halloumi, cut into 1.5cm-thick slices
- 400g ripe watermelon, cubed or balled with a melon baller
- 16–20 black Kalamata olives, pitted and roughly chopped
- 8 radishes, thinly sliced
- flour, for dusting
- light olive oil
- 1 tsp chilli flakes
- 30g pumpkin seeds, lightly toasted
- 2 tbsp finely chopped fresh mint

Dressing:
- 4 tbsp extra virgin olive oil
- 1 tbsp red wine vinegar
- juice of 1/2 lemon
- salt and freshly ground black pepper

Serves 4

Method:

1. Place the halloumi slices on a layer of kitchen paper, then place another layer of kitchen paper on top. Leave in the fridge for at least 1 hour. This will drain the briny liquid out of the cheese and allow for a crispier finish.
2. Arrange the watermelon, olives and radishes on a platter. Do this now, as you need to serve the halloumi hot from the BBQ.
3. **To make the dressing**, mix all the ingredients together and adjust the flavours to your taste – I like lots of lemon and black pepper.
4. Discard the kitchen paper and lightly dust the halloumi with flour, then brush with light olive oil.
5. Grill the halloumi on a hot BBQ until it's golden and crispy. Arrange the slices on the salad.
6. Drizzle over the dressing, but not too much on the watermelon, as it sucks it up like a sponge.
7. Sprinkle over the chilli flakes and scatter over the pumpkin seeds and mint.

Halloumi cheese is a traditional Cypriot cheese made with sheep or goat milk. It was first developed in the 4th century! It's a very firm, slightly 'squeaky' cheese that's at its best when grilled or fried, which gives it a golden, crispy crust and slightly yielding centre. Halloumi comes vacuum packed in brine, so it has a very long shelf life if kept in the fridge or freezer. It's ideal to have on hand, especially if you have unexpected vegetarian guests popping in!

Spinach, Artichoke, Olive and Feta Toasties

Ingredients:

- 2 tbsp olive oil, divided
- 1 onion, finely diced
- 2 cloves of garlic, crushed
- 1/2 tsp ground nutmeg
- 500g baby spinach
- 100g feta cheese, cubed
- 100g mozzarella, grated
- 20 Kalamata olives, pitted
- 6 marinated artichoke hearts, drained and halved
- 4–6 pita pockets (whole-wheat if preferred)
- 30g butter, melted
- Greek salad (p. 000), to serve

Serves 4

Method:

1. Heat 1 tablespoon of the olive oil in a large pan over a medium heat. Sauté the onion and garlic for 10 minutes, until softened. Add in the nutmeg and stir until fragrant.
2. Add handfuls of spinach to the pot and stir until it's just wilted – do not overcook. Drain off any liquid. Mix in the feta, mozzarella, olives and artichoke hearts.
3. Make a small slit along the edge of each pita pocket and stuff with the filling.
4. Mix the melted butter with the remaining 1 tablespoon of olive oil. Lightly brush the stuffed pita with the melted butter and oil. Toast on a medium-hot grill until golden brown.
5. Serve hot with a Greek salad.

Pita bread is a traditional flatbread enjoyed across the Mediterranean, from Cyprus to the Balkans. Pita pockets are hollow inside and make the perfect envelope to stuff with koftas, salads, cold meats – almost anything you please! You can find half-baked pita or vacuum-packed pitas that have a long shelf life. They're the ideal Pantry Pal for BBQs and lunchbox fillers. Choose whole-wheat pita bread for extra goodness and texture.

Fresh 'n' Cool Greek Salad

Ingredients:

- 1/2 red onion, very finely sliced
- juice and zest of 1–2 lemons
- 1 cucumber, diced or sliced into half moons
- 250g cherry tomatoes, halved
- 100g Kalamata olives
- 100g pistachio nuts, lightly toasted
- salt and freshly ground black pepper
- 4 pita pockets
- 100g plain feta cheese or Herby Chilli Marinated Feta (see p. 231), cubed
- extra virgin olive oil
- 1 cup fresh mint leaves, finely shredded

Serves 4

Method:

1. Place the sliced red onion in a bowl and pour over the lemon juice. Allow to 'pickle' for 10 minutes to tone down the astringent flavour of the onions.
2. Mix the cucumber, cherry tomatoes, Kalamata olives and pistachio nuts together in a large bowl and season with salt and pepper. Add the onion and lemon juice and mix through the salad.
3. Lightly toast the pita pockets on the BBQ or under the grill.
4. Arrange the salad and toasted pita pockets on a platter or 4 plates. Lift the feta out of its marinade and spoon it over the salad, then drizzle with the marinade.
5. Sprinkle over the lemon zest, drizzle over some olive oil and garnish with the fresh mint.

Kalamata olives are the firm black olives named after the city of Kalamata and they're synonymous with Greek food. They're the perfect olive to put out as a nibble with drinks, in salads or to add to cooked recipes. They're preserved in brine or olive oil, so they're an ideal Pantry Pal. I buy mine from the market so that I can sample them before I buy – I'm very fussy when it comes to olives!

Grilled Aubergine Salad with Pomegranate Seeds and Tahini Dressing

Ingredients:

- 4 aubergines
- salt and freshly ground black pepper
- 75ml olive oil
- 1 pomegranate, seeded
- 200g feta cheese
- 4 tbsp chopped fresh flat-leaf parsley
- 4 tbsp chopped fresh mint

Tahini dressing:
- 175ml (3/4 cup) water
- 125ml (1/2 cup) tahini
- juice of 1 lemon
- 1 clove of garlic, crushed
- salt and freshly ground black pepper

Serves 4

Method:

1. Wash the aubergine and slice into approximately 1cm-thick slices. Sprinkle with salt and layer the slices in a colander in the sink. Allow to stand for 15 minutes to draw out some of the moisture. Rinse in cold water and pat dry.
2. Brush both sides of the aubergine slices with a little olive oil and season well with salt and pepper. Cook on a hot grill until both sides are golden, slightly charred and have started to wrinkle.
3. To make the tahini dressing, whisk together all the ingredients for the dressing and adjust the seasoning to your liking. I often add extra lemon juice, as I love the tart taste with the nuttiness of the tahini.
4. Arrange the grilled aubergines on a platter and drizzle over a little of the dressing – you can serve extra on the side. Scatter over the pomegranate seeds, crumble over the feta and sprinkle the fresh herbs from a height to get an even scattering.
5. Serve warm as a salad or serve leftovers in a pita pocket with crunchy lettuce and extra dressing.

Tahini is a sesame seed paste that's widely used in Mediterranean and Middle Eastern cooking. It's one of the main ingredients in hummus, baba ganoush and halva, for example. You can buy it in glass jars from health food shops and speciality shops. Give it a good stir to mix in the oil, as it settles on the top. It's delicious spread on rye bread with a drizzle of honey or in smoothies.

Herby Chilli Marinated Feta

Ingredients:

- 4 cloves of garlic, crushed
- 2 bay leaves
- 1/2 red chilli, very finely chopped
- 250ml (1 cup) extra virgin olive oil
- juice and zest of 1 lemon
- 2 tsp dried oregano
- 2 tsp dried mint
- 1 tsp sugar
- 1 tsp pink peppercorns, crushed in a pestle and mortar
- 400g feta cheese, diced into cubes

Makes 1 large jar

Method:

1. Preheat the oven to 150°C. Remove the rubber seal from a large Kilner jar. Wash the jar and seal in hot soapy water and rinse well in fresh water. Place the jar upside down on the oven shelf and bake for 10 minutes, until it's dry and sterilised.
2. Mix together all the ingredients except the feta in a separate jar with a lid and shake very well. Place half the feta cheese in the Kilner jar and pour over half the marinade. Add the rest of the cheese and pour over the remainder of the marinade. Do not stir, as this will break up the cheese.
3. Leave to marinate for at least 1 day before serving. The feta will stay fresh for at least 1 week.

Feta cheese is a traditional cheese made with sheep or goat milk. The cheese is tightly compacted and stored in brine, which is best to keep it in to maintain its freshness. I love feta, as it's relatively low fat, keeps well and can be used in so many recipes. Try different fetas until you find your favourite one and it will become a Fresh Friend.

Lavender Shortbread with Lemon Cream

Ingredients:

- Lavender shortbread:
- 360g flour
- 90g cornflour
- 1 tsp baking powder
- pinch of salt
- 120g caster sugar
- 1 tbsp lavender flowers (fresh or dried), bashed in a mortar and pestle, or 2 tbsp lavender sugar
- 300g butter, chilled

Lemon cream:
- 150g caster sugar
- 600ml double cream
- juice and zest or 2 large lemons

Serves 6

Method:

1. Preheat the oven to 180°C. Lightly grease a rectangular Swiss roll tin.
2. Sift the flour, cornflour, baking powder and a pinch of salt together in a large bowl, then mix in the caster sugar and lavender.
3. Cut the butter into small cubes and add it to the bowl. 'Flutter' the mixture between your fingertips to rub the butter into the flour until it's completely mixed in. Alternatively, pulse together in a food processor until it forms a dough ball and 'chases' the blade. Do not overmix.
4. Press the dough into the prepared baking tin. Prick with the tines of a fork and bake for 25–30 minutes, until golden and firm to the touch.
5. Cut the shortbread into fingers in the tin, but allow to cool completely before trying to remove them.
6. **To make the lemon cream**, place the sugar and cream in a large pot on a low heat and slowly bring to the boil, stirring constantly. Boil for 3 minutes, then remove from the heat and cool. Add the lemon juice and zest and whisk well. Pour into 6 small jars or pots and chill for 3 hours.
7. Serve the lavender shortbread with the lemon cream and strong Greek coffee.

Lavender might seem like an odd ingredient in the kitchen, but it can be added to several dishes for an interesting twist. Crème brûlée topped with lavender sugar is a delight and lavender ice cream with melon preserve is a taste sensation. You can buy lavender sugar or bunches of dried lavender in farmers' markets.

Rose Petal Cosmopolitan

Ingredients:

- 25ml ouzo
- 1 tbsp triple sec
- Dash of rose syrup
- 50ml fresh lime juice
- 50ml pomegranate juice
- rose petals, to garnish

Serves 1

Method:

1. Mix all the ingredients in a cocktail shaker with ice.
2. Shake and strain into a chilled martini glass with.
3. Garnish with rose petals.

Peppermint Grape Iced Tea

Ingredients:

- 4 peppermint teabags, or 4 tbsp dried peppermint tea
- 1 litre boiling water
- 1/2 cup honey
- juice of 1/2 lemon
- 1 litre white grape juice, well chilled
- 2kg grapes, frozen overnight

Serves 8

Method:

1. Pour the boiling water over the peppermint tea and allow to infuse for 5 minutes.
2. Remove the tea bags or strain if using loose tea, stir in the honey to dissolve.
3. Pour in the grape and lemon juice and allow to cool for an hour. Transfer to the fridge until completely chilled.
4. Serve in chilled glasses with a small bunch of frozen grapes in each glass.

Chapter 10

American*ish*

Buffalo Chicken Sliders with Blue Cheese Mayonnaise

Ingredients:

- 500g chicken mince
- 60g butter, melted
- 2 cloves of garlic, crushed
- 1/2 stalk of celery, chopped
- 2 tsp Tabasco sauce
- 1 tsp paprika
- 1 tsp cayenne pepper
- 1/2 tsp English mustard powder
- 1/2 tsp white pepper
- sunflower oil

Blue cheese mayo:
- 100g blue cheese
- 175ml (3/4 cup) sour cream
- 80ml (1/3 cup) milk
- 80ml (1/3 cup) mayonnaise
- 1 tbsp red wine vinegar
- freshly ground black pepper

To serve:
- 6 mini burger buns, lightly toasted
- 2 heads of baby Cos or Little Gem lettuces, leaves separated

Makes 8 mini burgers

Method:

1. To make the blue cheese mayo, mix everything together until you get a fairly smooth dressing. Add a good pinch of black pepper if you like. Blue cheese is quite salty, so you probably won't need to add salt.
2. To make the chicken sliders, mix together all the ingredients except the sunflower oil with clean, wet hands, but do not overhandle. Divide into 8 balls and shape into firm, round burger patties. Cover and chill in the fridge for 1 hour to firm up.
3. Lightly oil the sliders with sunflower oil and place them on a medium-hot grill. Seal for 3–4 minutes before turning. If the burger sticks, it's not ready to turn.
4. Cook the burgers evenly on both sides for 12–15 minutes in total, until cooked through. Cut into the fattest part to check that there is no pink, undercooked meat.
5. Serve in a lightly toasted bun with blue cheese mayo and crunchy lettuce.

Tabasco is one of the most famous brand name hot sauces. It's ideal to use in cooking and also as a condiment. I particularly like to use it to add extra heat to a dish that needs it when I can't cook out more raw chilli or the graininess of ground spices. Try the other chilli flavours in the range, like jalapeño and chipotle.

Tex-Mex Steak Tacos with Corn Salsa

Ingredients:

- 4 sirloin or rump steaks

Marinade:
- 2 cloves of garlic, crushed
- 2 tbsp lime juice
- 1 tbsp olive oil
- 2 tsp ground cumin
- 1 tsp dried oregano
- 1 tsp cayenne pepper

Corn salsa:
- 1 x 340g tin of sweetcorn, drained
- 4 spring onions, finely sliced
- 1 large red pepper, diced
- 1 small red chilli, finely chopped
- juice of 1/2 lime
- 2 tbsp chopped fresh coriander
- 2 tsp extra virgin olive oil
- salt and freshly ground black pepper

To serve:
- 8 taco shells
- 100g (1 cup) grated Cheddar cheese
- 1 x 200ml tub of sour cream
- 4 tbsp chopped fresh coriander
- 4 limes, cut into wedges

Serves 4

Method:

1. Mix all the marinade ingredients together in a glass bowl. Add the steaks and move them around in the marinade until they're well coated. Cover, refrigerate and marinate for 1 hour.
2. Mix all the salsa ingredients together. Taste and season with salt, pepper and lime juice. Cover and set aside to infuse.
3. Remove the steaks from the fridge and allow to reach room temperature.
4. Grill the steaks on a hot BBQ for 3–4 minutes per side for rare to medium rare. This is the optimum way to cook these steaks, but if you want them medium to well done, move them to a cooler part of the BBQ and cook further. When they're done, allow the steaks to rest on a warm plate loosely covered with foil for 5 minutes.
5. Heat up the taco shells in a foil parcel on the grill.
6. Slice up the steak and allow each guest to fill the tacos with their choice of fillings: steak, salsa, grated cheese, sour cream, coriander and a squeeze of lime juice.

Cumin and its best pal, coriander, are probably the most used spices in my kitchen. I keep the whole seeds and the ground spice for different recipes. A warm, aromatic spice, cumin is used in Mediterranean, Mexican, Indian, Asian and Middle Eastern recipes, so it will definitely get a few outings when you cook from my books.

BBQ Turkey Breast with Peach Cranberry Relish

Ingredients:

- 2 turkey breasts or
  4 chicken supremes
- salt and freshly ground
  black pepper
- 30g butter, melted
- 2 tbsp apricot jam, gently
  melted in a pot
- green salad, to serve

Peach cranberry relish:
- 1 tbsp olive oil
- 1 onion, finely chopped
- 6 fresh peaches, pitted and sliced
- 1 large sprig of rosemary
- 100g dried cranberries
- 250ml (1 cup) apple cider vinegar
- 2 tbsp honey
- 1 tbsp dark brown sugar
- 1 tsp Worcestershire sauce
- salt and freshly ground
  black pepper

Serves 4

Method:

1. To make the peach cranberry relish, heat the olive oil in a pot over a medium heat. Gently sauté the onion for 8 minutes, until it's soft and translucent. Add the rest of the ingredients and gently bring up to the boil. Reduce the heat and cook down for 20 minutes, until thickened.
2. Season the turkey well with salt and pepper. Baste with the melted butter and apricot jam. Seal the skin side on a hot BBQ until it's crispy. Continue to seal all the sides well. Move to a medium-hot part of the BBQ and grill for 35–40 minutes, until cooked through, basting continually.
3. Serve with plenty of peach cranberry relish and a green salad.

Dried cranberries, or craisins, as they're called in the States, are one of my favourite Pantry Pals. They're delicious added to chicken or turkey stuffing, in wild rice and pecan nut salads and baked goods like scones. I like craisins in my porridge with a pinch of cinnamon.

Deconstructed BLT Salad

Ingredients:

- 1 tbsp olive oil
- 2 slices of brown sourdough or rye bread
- pinch of cayenne pepper
- pinch of sea salt
- 8 streaky rashers
- 1 small head of crunchy lettuce, like romaine or Cos, leaves separated
- 150g cherry tomatoes, halved
- 2 tbsp chopped fresh chives

Dressing:
- 3 tbsp mayonnaise
- 1 tbsp apple cider vinegar
- 1 tsp sugar
- 1 tsp sunflower oil
- salt and freshly ground black pepper

Serves 4

Method:

1. Lightly oil the bread and season with cayenne pepper and salt. Toast on the grill until it's nice and crispy, then break apart into croutons.
2. Grill the bacon until it's nice and crispy. Drain on kitchen paper to remove excess fat.
3. Mix all the dressing ingredients together and season to taste. I like mine with a little more vinegar.
4. For a deconstructed salad, arrange the croutons, crispy bacon, lettuce, tomatoes and dressing artistically on a plate. Sprinkle over the chopped chives.

Cayenne pepper is part of the chilli family and ranges in heat depending on quality. Use it to add heat during cooking or a pinch as a condiment to your finished meal. I often pair it with fresh lemon juice when I feel a dish is lacking something but I can't put my finger on it. Cayenne pepper has many health benefits, but it may not agree with everyone.

Spicy Pepperoni Potato Salad

Ingredients:

- 500g baby potatoes, halved
- 200g spicy pepperoni or chorizo
- 2 red onions, sliced
- 2 tbsp red wine vinegar
- salt and freshly ground black pepper
- 100g feta cheese
- 4 tbsp chopped fresh flat-leaf parsley

Serves 6

Method:

1. Steam or boil the potatoes for 15–20 minutes, until tender. Drain well in a colander and transfer to a serving bowl.
2. Cut the pepperoni or chorizo into thick slices and sauté in a pan until the fat runs out.
3. Add the sliced red onion and cook for 5 minutes, until softened. Pour in the red wine vinegar to deglaze the pan. Allow it to bubble up for 1 minute.
4. Mix the pepperoni and onions with the just-cooked potatoes to coat well with the oil. Season with plenty of salt and pepper.
5. Garnish with chunks of feta and plenty of parsley.

Red wine vinegar is one of my essential Pantry Pals. It's lighter in flavour, more acidic, less sweet and less syrupy than balsamic vinegar. It's great for salad dressings, marinades, pickles and in tomato-based sauces. It's my secret ingredient in caramelised red onions and slow-cooked spiced red cabbage.

Lee-Ann's Broccoli and Bacon Salad

Ingredients:

- 250g bacon lardons
- 3 heads of broccoli
- 80g (1/2 cup) raisins
- 70g (1/2 cup) sunflower seeds

Dressing:
- 2 tbsp white wine vinegar
- 1 tbsp caster sugar
- 200ml crème fraîche
- 2 tbsp mayonnaise
- 2 tbsp sunflower oil

Serves 4

Method:

1. Fry the bacon lardons until crispy. Drain on kitchen paper to remove excess fat.
2. Trim the hard stems from the broccoli. Break the tops into florets and chop into small pieces about the size of a peanut. You may find it easier to use your fingers to break up the florets. This is key, as you want small, uniform pieces because the broccoli is served raw.
3. Add the raisins, sunflower seeds and cooked bacon.
4. To make the dressing, mix the vinegar and sugar together until the sugar dissolves. Add the crème fraîche, mayonnaise and sunflower oil.
5. Mix the dressing into the salad. The broccoli florets can clump together with dressing, so I use 2 forks to toss the salad.

Bacon lardons are a staple Freezer Friend in my house. They come in small square packages that are easy portion sizes and stack well. You can fry them from frozen, as they defrost quickly in the pan. Buy Italian pancetta or dry-cured bacon so that it goes nice and crispy; that's where the real pleasure lies. Let's be honest – good bacon just makes everything better.

Crunchy Crudités Platter

Ingredients:

- 8 baby carrots, peeled
- 2 heads of baby Cos lettuce, broken into separate leaves
- 1 red pepper, sliced
- 1 cucumber, sliced into sticks
- 150g sugar snap peas or mangetout
- 150g baby corn
- other vegetables to choose from: celery sticks, broccoli florets, cherry tomatoes

Herby ranch dressing:
- 1 clove of garlic, crushed
- 250ml (1 cup) buttermilk
- 50ml (1/4 cup) mayonnaise
- 3 tbsp sour cream
- 3 tbsp finely chopped fresh chives or flat-leaf parsley
- 4 tsp white wine vinegar
- 1 tsp Dijon mustard
- salt and freshly ground black pepper

Serves 4

Method:

1. Mix together all the dressing ingredients and season to taste. I like mine quite tart, so add a little more vinegar if you prefer. Cover and chill while you prep the vegetables.
2. Sugar snap peas, mangetout and broccoli florets benefit from being lightly steamed for 3 minutes, then plunged into ice water to refresh.
3. Remove the tough fibres of celery stalks by starting from one end of the celery, grabbing the strings and pulling down the lengths. Chop into long pieces.
4. Prepare all the other vegetables by washing them, peeling where necessary and cutting into manageable pieces for dipping.

White wine vinegar is another Pantry Pal that's essential for salad dressings, pickling and even some desserts. Malt vinegar is very harsh and is really only for chips! White wine vinegar has a milder, more neutral taste and will give your dressings and recipes the right amount of acidic flavour without other strong flavours, like a balsamic vinegar would.

Retro Ten Layer Salad

Ingredients:

- 1 small head of iceberg lettuce, finely shredded
- 2 red peppers, diced into small pieces
- 1 red onion, finely diced
- 1 x 400g tin of sweetcorn, drained
- 2 medium carrots, peeled and grated
- 250g streaky bacon, grilled and chopped into small pieces
- 500g frozen petit pois, left out to defrost for 1 hour, then drained
- 200g (2 cups) grated Cheddar
- 100ml mayonnaise
- 3 tbsp dark brown sugar

Serves 8–10

Method:

1. Select a large glass bowl and start layering the ingredients: first the finely shredded lettuce, then the red pepper, red onion, sweetcorn, grated carrots, bacon bits and baby peas. Sprinkle over the cheese, then spread the mayonnaise evenly over the surface. If your bowl is very large, you may need an extra tablespoon of mayonnaise.
2. Cover and refrigerate for 1–2 hours. This salad is best made a few hours ahead for the flavours to infuse.
3. Just before serving, sprinkle the brown sugar evenly over the surface of the salad.

Frozen petit pois might seem like a mundane ingredient, but they're a real Freezer Treasure. Blitz with green chilli, lime and coriander for a fresh salsa, serve with bacon and croutons for a warm salad or purée with butter, mint and crème fraîche for modern mushy peas. Very far removed from school dinner peas!

Waldorf Salad Popcorn

Ingredients:

- 2 tbsp sunflower oil
- 220g (1 cup) popcorn kernels
- 3 stalks of celery
- sea salt
- 1 red apple, thinly sliced
- 250g seedless grapes
- 50g roasted cashew nuts
- 1 tbsp smoked paprika
- 60g butter, melted

Serves 4

Method:

1. Place a large pot on top of the BBQ and heat the sunflower oil in it. Add one kernel of popcorn to test the heat of the oil. When it pops, it's ready.
2. Add all the popcorn, cover the pot with a lid and wait until the popping stops.
3. Remove the tough fibres of the celery stalks by starting from one end of the celery, grabbing the strings and pulling down the lengths. Thinly slice the celery.
4. Season the popcorn well with salt, then mix through the celery, apple slices, grapes and cashews.
5. Sprinkle over the paprika and drizzle over the butter just before serving.

Forget microwave popcorn – real old-fashioned popcorn is where it's at for BBQs. It's cheap cheap and so quick as a snack to keep the hunger pangs at bay while you grill the meat. Experiment with different toppings: hot 'n' spicy for a savoury snack, or add Maltesers, melted butter and caramel for a sweet treat.

Salted Caramel Pseudo Banoffee

Ingredients:

- 250ml (1 cup) caster sugar (use your measuring jug to measure by volume)
- 175ml (3/4 cup) double cream
- 50g butter
- 1 tsp coarse salt

To serve:
- rich tea or coconut biscuits
- sliced banana

Makes 250ml

Method:

1. Remove the rubber seal from a 250ml glass jar and wash the jar in hot soapy water. Rinse very well in clean water and place upside on the oven shelf. Bake for 10 minutes at 150°C to dry and sterilise the jar.
2. Pour the sugar into a heavy-based pot and add 50ml (1/4 cup) water. Gently heat on a medium-low heat, without stirring, until the sugar dissolves. Do not stir or it can develop a candy floss-like texture.
3. Once the sugar has dissolved, crank up the heat and bring it to a boil. The sugar syrup will change from pale yellow to golden, gradually getting darker.
4. Remove the pot from the heat as soon as it turns a dark amber colour. Carefully whisk in the cream and then the butter – the mixture will bubble up. Once the butter has melted, add the salt.
5. Bottle the salted caramel immediately in the hot, sterilised jar. It will keep for up to 2 weeks in the fridge.
6. Once cooled, served with biscuits and sliced bananas.

Good salt is essential in any kitchen. I only use the cheap, fine, free-flowing salt for baking. Otherwise, it's coarse sea salt or pink Himalayan salt all the way, especially in BBQ – coarse salt helps to form a good crust on the food. I keep loose salt and a grinder that's set on a coarse grind.

Arabella's Triple Chocolate S'mores Board

Ingredients:

- 1 bag of pink and white marshmallows
- 1 bag of coconut marshmallows
- 2 packets of biscuits such as rich tea, coconut or plain digestives
- 250g fresh raspberries

Mars bar sauce:
- 1 x 397g tin of condensed milk
- 1 large Mars bar

White chocolate sauce:
- 200ml cream
- 200g white chocolate
- 1 tsp vanilla extract

Dark chocolate sauce:
- 100ml cream
- 200g dark chocolate (75% cocoa)

Serves 12

Method:

1. Soak 24 bamboo skewers in water for 1 hour.
2. To make the Mars bar sauce, place a glass bowl over a pot of simmering water, then pour the condensed milk into the bowl. Break the Mars bar into the condensed milk and heat until it's mostly melted. Some bits of caramel may stay whole, but that's part of the fun.
3. To make the white chocolate sauce, place a glass bowl over a pot of simmering water. Pour in the cream and heat it up. Just as the cream starts to bubble, take the pot off the hob and break the white chocolate into the hot cream. Add the vanilla extract and allow to sit for 5 minutes before stirring.
4. To make the dark chocolate sauce, place a glass bowl over a pot of simmering water. Pour in the cream and heat it up. Just as it's about to bubble, break in the dark chocolate. Keep it on a low simmer and stir until it's smooth and glossy.
5. At the end of the BBQ, thread lots of marshmallows onto the bamboo skewers and toast them to your liking. Sandwich them between 2 biscuits, then pull the toasted marshmallows off the skewer.
6. You can then dip the sandwiched marshmallow biscuit in one of the three chocolate sauces. Fresh berries like raspberries are also delicious in the mix.
7. Have fun!

Good-quality 75% cocoa dark chocolate is essential, not only to enjoy as is, but to temper and cook with. Please don't buy 'cooking' chocolate, it's hideous. What you need is couverture chocolate, which has the right amount of cocoa butter and is made so that you can melt and temper the chocolate. Eating chocolate often contains vegetable oils and other additives that can cause the chocolate to split and curdle.

Cookies and Cream Boozy Milkshake

Ingredients:

- 50ml bourbon
- 2 tsp dark crème de cacao
- 2 tsp white crème de cacao
- 100ml milk
- 50ml cream
- 2 scoops vanilla ice cream
- 1 chocolate cookie

Serves 1

Method:

1. Put all the ingredients in a blender and blend until smooth.
2. Pour into a tall glass and serve with a straw.
3. Garnish with a chocolate cookie.

Camomile Vanilla Iced Tea

Ingredients:

- 4 camomile tea bags or 4 tbsp of loose camomile tea
- 1 litre of boiling water
- 1/2 cup honey
- 1 tsp vanilla paste or beans of 1/2 vanilla pod (don't use extract)
- juice of 1 lime
- lime wedges, to serve
- fresh mint, to serve
- ice cubes, to serve

Serves 8

Method:

1. Pour the boiling water over the tea and allow to infuse for 5 minutes.
2. Remove the tea or strain if using loose tea. Stir in the honey to dissolve.
3. Allow to cool for an hour then move to the fridge to cool down completely.
4. Stir in the vanilla and lime juice.
5. Serve over ice with lime wedges and fresh mint leaves.

TOP Ways of BBQ'ing
Fruit and Veggies

When we think of BBQ, it's normally meat, meat, meat, and more meat. But BBQ'd fruits and vegetables are absolutely delicious and even turn under ripe fruit into a caramelised treat. After a meat fest BBQ of burgers, rashers, chicken and steak, a refreshing dessert or warm salad of BBQ'd fruit not only cleanses the palate, but can actually aid digestion of fats and proteins.

Clean your BBQ grill well of charred debris, rub with half a lemon to sanitise, and you are ready to grill the fruit. Lightly brush the fruit with sunflower oil and sprinkle over dark brown sugar to add extra caramelised gooeyness. This will work well with slightly under-ripe fruit, as grilling helps to bring out the natural sweetness of fruit. So a hard mango or pineapple will be greatly enhanced by BBQ'ing. You can mix the BBQ'd fruit with fresh fruit like strawberries. Serve with finely chopped mint and yoghurt, or mix through a savoury salad.

Banana
To BBQ: Leave the skin on, slice lengthways and BBQ skin down until the banana is soft. Sprinkle over a little sugar, ground cinnamon and a squeeze of lemon. A good match with a drizzle of rum!

Mango
To BBQ: Peel the mango, and slice a mango 'cheek' from either side of the mango pit. Lightly oil with sunflower oil and and grill until slightly charred. Serve with fresh limes.

Papaya
To BBQ: Slice in half lengthways and scoop out the black seeds. Generously squeeze with lime juice and add a little finely chopped stem ginger in syrup to the cavity. BBQ until slightly softened.

Peaches
To BBQ: Halve using the pit as your guide. Remove the pit and surrounding woody bits. Lightly brush with amaretto liqueur, melted butter and sprinkle over brown sugar and BBQ.

Pineapple
To BBQ: Peel the pineapple and chop into large chunks, discarding the fibrous middle core. Lightly oil with chilli oil, BBQ and serve with sea salt, desiccated coconut and lime juice.

Grapes
To BBQ: Take a bunch of seedless grapes and lightly oil them with a light olive oil or grapeseed oil. BBQ on a medium hot BBQ until they just start to blister and burst. Serve with cheese.

Figs
To BBQ: Break the figs in half and lightly oil with with a light olive oil. BBQ on a medium hot grill until they just start to char. Serve with balsamic vinegar reduction and mascarpone.

Summer BBQs needn't be just about burgers and meat, veggies on the BBQ take on a whole new smokey flavour and crunchy texture. Lightly oil with an oil like grape seed, sunflower or light olive oil which don't burn as easily as extra virgin olive oil. Use these tender char-grilled vegetables to stuff into pita pockets with hummus and tzatziki or add to baby salad leaves for a delicious warm salad.

Globe Artichoke

To BBQ: Buy bottled artichoke hearts marinated in oil, often sold in garlic and herb flavoured oil. Lift out of the oil and shake off the excess. Keep the flavoured oil to make salad dressing. BBQ on a fine mesh overlay BBQ grill so that the pieces don't fall through the grill.

Asparagus

To BBQ: Chop off the very woody tips. Lightly oil with grape seed, sunflower or light olive oil and BBQ until slightly charred. Goes well with lots of lemon juice, black pepper and Parmesan shavings.

Aubergine

To BBQ: Slice into thin 1cm slices. Very lightly oil and cook over a hot flame until charred. Excellent with a little curry powder sprinkled over before grilling.

Butternut Squash

To BBQ: Leave the skin on or peel, and scoop out the seeds. Boil or steam for 5 minutes. Pat dry and lightly oil before grilling. Sprinkling over a little garam masala or fennel seeds before grilling enhances the lovely flavour of the squash.

Courgettes

To BBQ: Top and tail and cut into 1cm thick slices lengthways. Use a good knife and mind your fingers. Lightly oil and grill until charred. Squeeze over a little lemon when cooked.

Portobello Mushrooms

To BBQ: Lightly oil and grill on a slightly cooler part of the BBQ as they will take a little longer and you don't want them to dry out. Delicious with a dollop of basil or sun-dried tomato pesto.

Red Peppers

To BBQ: Chop the bottom off, turn upside down onto the stem and slice off the four 'walls'. Lightly oil and BBQ until charred and soft. Top with hummus or cream cheese and chives like a slice of bread.

TopFruit.com

263

Cooking with Calor
this BBQ Season

At Calor, we want to ensure that you have all the tools and information at your fingertips to make the very best of the BBQ season, to show off your chef skills while at the same time making sure you and those around you are safe!

To ensure you enjoy all of the delicious BBQ recipes in Relish in style, Calor has launched a new innovation in outdoor cooking, the Calor Mini-BBQ. This clever piece of essential cooking equipment is lightweight, stylish and highly portable. It's also easy to use whether you want to BBQ in style at home or enjoy superior gas cooking on the go, anytime, anywhere!

BBQs are extremely popular particularly during the warmer months but they can also become potentially dangerous when mixed with carelessness or excessive alcohol. The combination of a party atmosphere, drinks flowing freely, children playing and an open fire can quickly cause a tragic accident. Simple precautions, pre-planning and care, especially regarding young children is vital. Calor do not want to stop the fun, but make sure that you have the very best BBQ experience with your family and friends.

Though before you get started with these great recipes, take some time to read through the following tips.

Tips for a having a safe BBQ

- Ensure that your barbecue is serviced and maintained correctly including scheduled pressure testing of any gas cylinders and checking of the condition of all hoses and connections.
- Carry out a check of the cylinder for rust or damage and ensure any connections are correctly tightened on gas barbecue before lighting
- Always site a BBQ on a firm, level base sheltered from wind gusts and well away from anything flammable like garden sheds, vegetation, fences etc
- Have a garden hose or similar continuous supply of water available at all times
- Follow the manufacturer's instructions and use the correct start up and shut down procedures
- Ensure that the lit barbecue is in the care of a responsible adult at all times
- Never put any flammable liquid on a barbecue
- Keep children away from any BBQ and remember to remove and secure any lighters and matches
- Only use a barbecue in a well-ventilated area as fumes and gases emitted may be harmful
- If a gas leak does occur shut off the cylinder immediately and allow any gas to dissipate

Always remember the following fire safety tips, and put them in a place easy to reach!

- Remember that LPG is flammable, heavier than air and may remain in areas for some time
- You may want to consider having a fire extinguisher nearby for emergencies
- Use alcohol responsibly around barbecue
- Clear the surrounding area of combustibles before lighting a barbecue
- Allow hot ashes or coals to cool for 48 hours before removing them
- Home fire safety is important for the whole family and preparation can prevent a tragedy

❝

BBQ should be fun and involve good food, family and friends but safety is key

Safe Storage of Your Calor Gas Cylinder

- Store gas bottles outdoors in a well-ventilated space
- Gas cylinders should never be stored indoors.
- Gas cylinder should always be stored upright.
- Do not store gas cylinders near an ignition source.
- If you store your BBQ or patio heater indoors, when not in use, you should always detach the gas bottle first and store it separately outdoors.

Where to Place Your BBQ for Use

- Adequate ventilation is essential when using a BBQ to allow the gas to burn and burnt gases to dissipate.
- BBQs should never be used near flammable objects.
- BBQs should NEVER be used indoors because of the risk of toxic fumes, smoke or even fire.
- Keep children safely away from BBQs and gas bottles.

Checking Your LPG Gas BBQ

The leading cause of BBQ fires is equipment failure, leaks or breaks

- Use the correct type of hose. Do not make temporary connections. Keep hose gently curved to prevent kinks and damage.
- Cracked or damaged hoses and/or gas regulators should be replaced before use.
- Check hoses to make sure they have not perished by applying soapy water and checking for bubbles.
- Check hoses for blockages, such as spiders, which might have nested inside during winter.
- Check connections to make sure that they are clean and fitting snugly.

Operating Your BBQ Gas Cylinder

- Keep the gas cylinder upright and on a stable base.
- When done using your BBQ, turn off at the gas cylinder first and then at the BBQ controls.
- Always turn off the gas bottle valve when you're not using your BBQ.
- Remember, adequate ventilation is essential.
- Shut off the bottle valve before disconnecting the bottle from the BBQ, even if you think the bottle is empty.
- A safety valve is fitted to the vapour space to allow automatic relief of any excess pressure due to overfilling, or in the event of a fire.
- Never tamper with the safety valve or other gas bottle fittings. Do not use undue force to open or close the main cylinder valve.

So follow these simple steps and have a great experience this BBQ season! To check out the new Calor Mini-BBQ, and how you can easily set it up at home or on the go with the 400g gas cartridge or the 6kg lightweight patio gas cylinder, scan this QR code or visit our website at **calorgas.ie/living**

CALOR
now you can

Top Tips for a Tasty (and safe) barbecue

From casual family dinners to easy or relaxed entertaining with friends, a barbecue is the perfect way to spend an evening (weather permitting). But just because you are cooking outdoors, don't let your good habits in the kitchen go up in smoke when you light the barbecue – you want your friends, family and neighbours to go home with memories of a good time, not a tummy bug to remember you by! To make the most of the chance to cook outdoors, here are some top tips from safefood for how to get it right every time.

Before you get grilling

Before you begin to set up your barbecue this year and think of your menu, give your barbecue grill a thorough clean by scrubbing the metal rack with a suitable oven cleaner or a damp brush dipped in bicarbonate of soda. And remember to rinse it thoroughly with warm, soapy water afterwards.

Keeping your cool

When cooking and eating outdoors, food is away from your fridge for a longer period of time which can lead to germs multiplying quickly. With this in mind, keep perishable foods like salads coleslaw and quiche in your fridge until you need them.

Before you start

Before you try your best imitation of your favourite TV chef, make sure frozen foods are fully thawed (preferably in the fridge on the bottom shelf; which may take overnight) before you start cooking them. Keep foods you plan to cook properly chilled in the fridge or a cool box until needed and light your barbecue well in advance; for charcoal barbecues, the flames should have died down before you start cooking.

It's in your hands

As with preparing any food, make sure to wash your hands before and after handling food. Remember to keep raw meat separate from cooked meat and ready-to-eat foods like salads. Always use separate utensils for handling raw and cooked meat when cooking. Never put cooked food on a dish that has been used for raw meat or poultry (unless it's been thoroughly washed in between) and keep food covered whenever possible.

Cook with confidence!

The big issue when barbecuing is making sure your food has been cooked thoroughly, all the way through. This is particularly important when cooking poultry, pork, minced and skewered meats, such as burgers, sausages and kebabs on the barbecue - while the outside may look cooked (and in some cases burnt), the inside can still be raw.

safefood recommends these meats should be cooked until they are piping hot all the way through, with no pink meat remaining and the juices run clear. If you've got lots of people visiting your barbecue and want to ensure that meat is thoroughly cooked, why not pre-cook the meat in your kitchen just before you put it on the barbecue for that great flavour.

When cooking foods on the barbecue make sure to turn them regularly and move them around the grill to ensure they ares cooked evenly on all sides – then remove them from the heat and place themon a clean plate. For meats that need to be cooked all the way through be sure to cut into the centre of them to check that:

- They are piping hot all the way through

- There is no pink meat left and

- The juices run clear

Steaks or whole meat joints of beef or lamb can be served 'rare' as long as they are cooked on the outside as any harmful bacteria will be on the outside only, and not in the centre.

Mind that marinade!

If you like to marinate your meat, make sure any marinade used on raw meat is not then used as a sauce to coat vegetables or cooked meat as it will contain raw meat bacteria! If you want to use marinade as a sauce, be sure to cook it in a saucepan and bring it to a rolling boil before serving it.

Love those leftovers

If there are any leftovers from your barbecue, these should not be left outside where they may be in the sun and where insects and animals might be able to access them. As with all leftovers, cover these foods and allow them to cool in a cool place (the kitchen) before refrigerating within 2 hours of cooking. The rule to remember for leftovers is - if in doubt, throw them out.

7 golden rules for a safe barbecue

1   Keep perishable foods like salads, coleslaw and quiche in your fridge until you are about to serve them.

2   Burgers, sausages and kebabs, pork and poultry must be cooked all the way through - but steaks or whole meat joints of beef or lamb can be served 'rare' as harmful bacteria are on the outside only (and not in the centre).

3   If you like to marinate your meat, make sure any marinade used on raw meat is not then used as a sauce to coat vegetables or cooked meat as it will contain raw meat bacteria.

4   If you choose to barbecue any frozen food, it must be completely thawed on the bottom shelf of your fridge before you cook it.

5   When handling raw meat and poultry, wash your hands thoroughly and frequently, most importantly before going on to prepare saladsand other ready to eat foods..

6   Once your meat is cooked thoroughly, make sure to keep cooked meat separate from raw meat and to use separate chopping boards, cooking utensils and plates. Harmful bacteria in raw meat, poultry and their juices can cross contaminate cooked food and lead to food poisoning, something your guests won't thank you for.

7   If there are leftovers from your barbecue, allow the food to cool before refrigerating, however make sure to refrigerate food within two hours of cooking. Always remember that with leftovers - if in doubt, throw it out.

For more information on food safety and healthy eating including recipes, visit www.safefood.eu and enjoy your barbecue, whatever the weather!

Chi Chi Iced Teas

My love of interesting, exotic ingredients extends into the world of cocktails, bubbly, fine wine, seriously good coffee and teas, tissanes and infusions of every variety. When I was creating cocktails and non alcoholic coolers for each country, I thought it would be fun to base them on chilled herbal infusions. Iced teas give you a wonderful flavour base to build on, and are very refreshing and thirst quenching.

Chamomile Tea
Chamomile is a flowering herb and it is the dried flowers that we infuse with boiling water to make a tea. The two main varieties of chamomile tea are Roman chamomile, Anthemis nobilis, and German chamomile, Matricaria chamomilla. I love the heady aroma and golden colour.

Earl Grey Tea
Earl Grey tea is a black tea which gets its wonderful citrusy flavour from from bergamot oil. Bergamot is a citrus fruit cultivated in the Mediterranean. The essential oil is extracted from the skin and added to the tea leaves imparting a bright, fresh flavour.

Chai Tea
Chai tea is a traditional spiced tea drink from India. A black tea is brewed with a blend of aromatic spices such as cinnamon, cardamom, ginger and cloves and then sweetened. Hot or frothed milk is added to the tea for a rich, creamy, fragant drink.

Green Tea
Green tea, like black and oolong teas, is made from the leaves of the Camellia sinensis plant. To make black and oolong teas, the leaves are fermented. In green tea, the leaves are steamed which gives the tea a completely different taste, colour and aroma and also retains more healthy compounds.

Hibiscus Tea
Hibiscus tea is made from dried Hibiscus scarifier flowers which are infused with boiling water to create a deeply coloured red tea, with a lovely fragrance and flavour. It is caffeine free and can be enjoyed hot or cold. You can also get hibiscus flowers preserved in syrup, fun for cocktails.

Irish Breakfast Tea
Irish breakfast tea is a full-bodied, robust tea with a rich colour and taste. It is a blend of several types of black teas, most often Assam, Rwandan and Darjeeling teas. This creates a maltier, stronger flavoured tea than say a Ceylon style tea. Enjoyed black, with milk and also sugar.

Lemon grass
Unlike other teas where the leaf is infused, to make a lemongrass tea you need to decoct the woody stem. This is done by first bruising it to release the flavours, then simmering vigorously to extract the flavour. Other ingredients like ginger and mint can be added.

Peppermint Tea
Peppermint tea is made by steeping the dried leaves and stems of the Mentha piperita plant in boiling water. Morocco is famous for its mint tea where it is brewed using fresh mint leaves and green tea. Serving this tea is an integral part of their hospitality and social customs.

Rooibos Tea
Rooibos, also known as red bush or bush tea, is made from the leaves and bark of South African bush. Rooibos has a distinctive deep red colour, heady aroma and naturally sweet taste. Caffeine free, and antioxidant rich, you can serve it with milk and sugar or honey and lemon.

Yerba Maté Tea
This is a popular South American beverage made by steeping the leaves and stems of the yerba maté plant in boiling water. It is traditionally drunk from a gourd and through a metal straw. There are several varieties available, some which are served with milk and sugar and others flavoured with orange peel.

◄Visit thegibsonhotel.ie

the gibson hotel